THE PUBLIC-PRIVATE PARTNERSHIP MODEL:

IDENTIFYING SECURITY BEST PRACTICES FOR CRITICAL

INFRASTRUCTURE

by

Mathias R. Plass

A Dissertation Presented in Partial Fulfillment

of the Requirements for the Degree

Doctor of Science in Cyber Security

CAPITOL TECHNOLOGY UNIVERSITY

May 2015

THE PUBLIC-PRIVATE PARTNERSHIP MODEL:

IDENTIFYING SECURITY BEST PRACTICES FOR CRITICAL

INFRASTRUCTURE

by

Mathias R. Plass

May 2015

Approved:

Dr. Emily Darraj, Chair/Mentor

Dr. Matt Fischer, Committee

Dr. Robert Herschbach, Committee

Accepted and Signed: _Dr. Emily Darraj_ _May 2, 2015_
Dr. Emily Darraj                   Date

Accepted and Signed: _____ _May 2, 2015_
Dr. Matt Fischer                   Date

Accepted and Signed: _Robert Herschbach_ _May 2, 2015_
Dr. Robert Herschbach              Date

_____ _May 2, 2015_
Helen G. Barker, DM                Date
Dean, School of Business and Information Sciences
Capitol Technology University

# ABSTRACT

The basis of this qualitative case study was to determine how security frameworks designed utilizing the public-private partnership model aid in the identification of suggested security best practices for a telecommunications provider's critical infrastructure within the United States. The themes generated during the completion of this study-enforced ways that critical infrastructure partner organizations could identify suggested security best practices. These themes also opened up additional avenues for future research surrounding additional methods for identifying suggested security best practices such as security awareness and education. This research also established that opportunities exist for the development of additional suggested security best practices by expanding the population to include additional critical infrastructure partners and larger sectors.

## DEDICATION

This is dedicated to my wonderful wife Kelley whose love, support, and constant motivation was instrumental in my completion of this endeavor. To my three wonderful children, Nathan, Kate, and Annaka, who let Daddy have the necessary time needed to work on this with limited distraction. I love you guys. Finally, to the two individuals who taught me that nothing in life worth having or pursuing is easily handed to people. You taught me that hard work pays and for that I am eternally grateful. I love you Mom and Dad.

# ACKNOWLEDGEMENTS

The doctoral process is a very long and at times difficult course for one to embark on. It can be a lonely and dark task at time but it is the individuals that you surround yourself with that become the bright beacons of light needed to make that process a success. During my quest there were several individuals that were often that beacon. Dr. Van Horn who provided the necessary guidance and direction to keep me on point; Dr. Herschbach who provided his expertise and found the numerous grammar stumbling blocks that one hits as they work continuously on the living document; and Dr. Darraj who provided guidance and support through some of the most difficult times. My most sincere thanks to the three of you as you all made this process less difficult and most rewarding.

I would also like to acknowledge and thank those faceless co-workers who took the times out of their busy day to sit with me and answer, at times, some extremely thought provoking questions around cybersecurity. Their willingness to go through this process with me allowed this process to gain great meaning and insight to the questions I endeavored to answer and gave them some new found context on what could be done to improve security and identify new suggested best practices to incorporate in their daily tasks.

TABLE OF CONTENTS

## List of Tables

# List of Figures

CHAPTER 1: INTRODUCTION

The purpose of this study was to determine how security frameworks designed utilizing the public-private partnership model aid in the identification of suggested security best practices for a telecommunications provider's critical infrastructure within the United States. To establish this, the study looked at three security frameworks designed using the public-private partnership model and ascertained if the current model should be changed and a new model designed. The Department of Homeland Security has determined there are sixteen critical sectors in the United States necessary for continual operations of the country, but for the purpose of this study, the focus was solely on a telecommunications provider within the communications sector (NIPP, 2010). This study begins with an overview of the public-private partnership model, starting with its historical beginnings and continuing through its usage in the Department of Homeland Security's National Infrastructure Protections Plan (NIPP Communications Sector Overview, 2010). This transition allowed the study to focus on the Homeland Security Presidential Directive 7 (HSPD-7). The HSPD-7 directive designed the protections around the sixteen critical infrastructures discussed within the National Infrastructure Protection Plan.

Kshetri and Murugesan (2013) discussed the current US strategy for protecting critical infrastructure. This strategy was primarily driven by the need to combat cybersecurity threats and centered on Presidential orders (2013). The main driver of the strategy comes from the public-private partnership model utilized in the National Infrastructure Protection Plan (NIPP, 2010). The intent of the National Infrastructure Protection Plan is to protect critical infrastructure using a collaborative approach between the sector partners, known as the public-private partnership model, which provides the unilateral appeal necessary for the model's success (Kshetri & Murugesan, 2013).

## Background of the Study

The protections surrounding critical infrastructures have been a priority of the United States government for more than a decade (McNamara, 2013). Since 9/11, the media headlines have been filled with news of cyber-attacks, cyber breaches, and cyber intrusions. Highlighting some of these headlines, Glennon (2012) spoke about the attack on Estonia's government systems in 2007; the Russian invasion of Georgia in 2008; and the 2009 breach of Google's email system and foreign hackers breaking into the United States national electric grid. These and other incidents demonstrate the growing use of cyber-attacks not only for personal gain and fame, but also as a precursor to conventional warfare (Glennon, 2012).

The use of cyber tactics in warfare is not just a concern among nations but the use of these new tactics as a disruption tool by terrorists (Goel, 2011). Before 9/11, cyber-attacks were minimal distractions that would simply deface websites or cause denial of service attacks, inconveniencing users. The use of cyber-attacks in Estonia and Georgia has highlighted the growing concern of critical attacks on infrastructure necessary to run and protect a country (Goel, 2011). The concern now to the United States is how government should go about protecting critical infrastructure and the method of choice by the Department of Homeland Security was to utilize the public-private partnership model (NIPP, 2010).

The National Infrastructure Protection Plan seeks to protect sixteen of the most critical infrastructures within the United States. For the purposes of this study, three of the security frameworks designed using the public-private partnership model, as it relates to a telecommunications provider within the communications sector, were evaluated. Alcaraz and Zeadally (2013) stated critical infrastructures are those interconnected sets of systems and assets that support daily activities such as banking, travel, power consumption, and communications. The disruption of these critical infrastructures and services could cause social and economic consequences at the national level because these services are so interdependent upon one another (2013).

The significance of this study to critical infrastructure protection was in determining how security frameworks designed using the public-private partnership model aid in identifying suggested security best practices to protect critical systems. The National Security Agency (NSA) conducted a study from 2009 to 2011 on the number of cyber-attacks within the United States upon critical infrastructures and found there was a 17-fold increase over the study period (Alcaraz & Zeadally, 2013). The Department of Homeland Security's Industrial Control System Cyber Emergency Response Team (ICS-CERT) who conducted a similar survey over the same period found a 20-fold increase in the number of incidents outside organizations required the government's assistance in correcting, further reinforcing the NSA study (2013). To understand the effects of these cyber-attacks on critical infrastructure the motivation of the attackers needs to be determined (Alcaraz and Zeadally, 2013). To do this cyber attackers were classified into four groups (2013):

- Technically Skilled – those cyber attackers using their abilities to expose a system's vulnerabilities
- Cybercriminals – those cyber attackers who wish to disrupt services purely for financial gain
- State-Sponsored – those cyber attackers involved in cyber-espionage

- General Cyber Attackers – those cyber attackers who are driven by political or religious beliefs; i.e. organizations such as al-Qaeda or Anonymous

Attackers falling under one of these classifications can subject the communications sector, as well as other critical sectors, to numerous attacks (Alcaraz & Zeadally, 2013). These threats can involve attacks to an organization's dial-up and broadband communications through attack methods such as war-dialing, password cracking, replay attacks, spoofing or a host of many others (2013). Attacks on an organization's wireless communications system, such as deliberate exposure attacks, sniffing, traffic analysis and integrity attacks, could cause loss of faith in services provided to the organization's customers (2013). These attacks can seriously disrupt critical services not only to citizens of the United States but also to its first-responders in times of need (2013).

The study determined how security frameworks designed using the public-private partnership model aid in identifying suggested security best practices for the protection of critical infrastructure, in particular the telecommunications systems critical to the United States. Podbregar and Podbregar (2012) described the public sector as any entity that creates and delivers public policy, manages the public's resources, is accountable to those resources, and accepts the risks to those public critical infrastructures. Meidute and Paliulis (2011) stated the responsibility for the development of an infrastructure provides the necessary services and creates favorable conditions and controls to operate the infrastructure to its fullest potential. The effectiveness of the public and private sectors working together highlights the strength of the partnership.

The purpose of this study was to determine how the security frameworks designed using the public-private partnership model aid in allowing a seamless collaboration between the critical infrastructure partners in the creation of suggested security best practices. It also aided in determining if the existing model needs only a revision or if a new model needs to be created for the future to protect the United States' critical infrastructures. To determine if the model aids in identifying suggested security best practices this study looked at security frameworks designed using the model such as the P3 Equilibrium Framework model created by Garvin in 2007 and modified by Garvin and Bosso in 2008. It will also look at the Cyber Terrorism Framework introduced by Ahmad and Yunos in 2012. Finally, the study will look at the National Institute of Standards and Technology's (NIST) Cybersecurity Framework model introduced in February 2014.

The NIST Cybersecurity Framework was designed out of a need to better protect critical infrastructure within the United States and is outlined in the National Infrastructure Protection Plan Revision of 2013 (NIPP, 2013). It needs to be determined with this study if any of the three previously discussed frameworks provide the necessary groundwork in determining whether or not the public-private partnership model is the proper model in identifying suggested security best practices to protect critical infrastructure or if future research will be needed to design a new model. If the model aids in identifying suggested security best practices, then the future work section will look to outline ways the model can be further used for suggested security best practice creation to protect critical infrastructure against new and emerging threats.

## Statement of the Problem

The general problem, according to Newmeyer (2012), is the United States Government has failed to address growing cybersecurity issues. Westby (2012) similarly stated Congress has struggled with cybersecurity issues for years, and Westby continued by specifically stating that Congress is currently in the dark in protecting critical infrastructures. The specific problem is private and public sector partners lack security best practices to protect critical infrastructure from cyberattack (Federal Register, 2013; IT SCC, 2013; McConnell, 2013; Wildman, 2013; Canfield and Ward, 2013; IT SCC, 2013; Rupy and Mayer, 2013; Chessen, Polk, Podey, Symons, and Harvie, 2013; Coffey, Srihari, and Scarpelli, 2013).

This dissertation used a qualitative exploratory case study. Interviews were utilized allowing the researcher to obtain information from employees within a critical infrastructure telecommunications provider; and allow the employees to have a voice in determining how security frameworks designed using the public-private partnership model aid in identifying suggested security best practices within their organization. The employees from this telecommunications provider provided representation to this qualitative research design. The use of interviews allowed the researcher of this study to determine how the security frameworks designed using the public-private partnership model aid in identifying suggested security best practices for protecting critical infrastructure within a telecommunications provider.

The general population for this study was varying employees from a critical infrastructure telecommunications provider from within the communications sector. The population for this research was segmented to include employees from the security team, Microsoft Windows server team, desktop support team, and the senior leadership team. The responses from these employees provided for a seamless view on suggested security best practice creation for critical infrastructure protection. The responses also determined whether the security frameworks designed using the public-private partnership model aid in identifying those suggested security best practices.

## Purpose of the Study

The purpose of this study was to determine how the security frameworks designed using the public-private partnership model aid in identifying suggested security best practices for a telecommunications provider's critical infrastructure within the United States. The research method selected for this dissertation was a qualitative exploratory case study, using interviews. This research design allowed for a qualitative analysis using interviews to solicit input from a critical infrastructure's employees. The reasons as to why an exploratory case study, using interviews, fit well within this study is while there is significant research around critical infrastructure there is a general lack or absence of academic research determining how security frameworks designed using the public-private partnership model aid in the identification of suggested security best practices. The usage of an exploratory case study, using interviews, allowed the researcher to explore a problem the data does not completely define (Stebbins, 2001).

The method of choice by the Department of Homeland Security to protect critical infrastructure security and resilience was to use the public-private partnership model (NIPP, 2013). The public-private partnership model has been utilized in several areas, one in particular is the transportation sector where the partnership model has aided in the completion of road and bridge projects and has been extremely successful (Garvin and Bosso, 2008). This study determined how the security frameworks designed using the public-private partnership model aid in the identification of suggested security best practices within a telecommunications provider. As this was a qualitative exploratory case study, unlike a quantitative case study, it did not perform an assessment on variables. The specific population utilized in this study was a representative selection of

8

fifteen employees from a telecommunications provider within the communications sector. The communications sector is listed as one of the sixteen critical infrastructures within the United States being studied to determine how security frameworks designed using the public-private partnership model aid in identifying suggested security best practices. The geographic locations for this study were centered on the telecommunications provider's primary information technology hubs. The first in Naperville, Illinois, the second in West Point, Georgia, and the third in Denver, Colorado. The researcher conducted the case study from a virtual environment for the participants in West Point, Georgia and Denver, Colorado but worked directly with participants from within the Naperville, Illinois location. It should also be noted that this telecommunications provider wishes to not have their name used in this study so henceforth this telecommunication provider will be known as "Company XYZ".

## Significance of the Study

The significance of this study is that it helped determine how security frameworks designed using the public-private partnership model aid in identifying suggested security best practices and are a good fit for the protection of Company XYZ's critical infrastructure. This study was unique in that there is currently little to no academic research surrounding how security frameworks designed using the public-private partnership models aid in the identification of suggested security best practices as it relates to critical infrastructure protection of telecommunications providers. Businesses and private entities within the communications sector are in competition on a daily basis and it seems very unlikely these businesses would be willing to freely share the security best practices of their business. This is primarily because most businesses consider their security best practices confidential and proprietary information and sharing these security practices could allow a competitor to have an unfair advantage against the other in the marketplace.

A further significance of this study was the knowledge gained would help raise the visibility of critical infrastructure protection. The protection of critical infrastructures within the United States has become increasingly more visible with the introduction of large amounts of malware, bot networks, and infiltration from terrorist networks, and rogue states to name just a few. For example, in early September 2014, a resourceful terrorist organization, ISIS (the Islamic State of Iraq and Syria), was found to be working in collaboration with Latin American drug cartels (Gaffney, 2014). This collaboration has already been seen in probing efforts on the critical electric grid where in June 2013 an improvised explosive was used to destroy an electric substation (Gaffney, 2014).

This study evaluated how security frameworks designed using the public-private partnership model aid in the identification of suggested security best practices and questioned whether the use of the public-private partnership model should continue in its current form or if the creation of a new model is necessary. The private sector can benefit from these results, as it can allow the private sector to help in the determination of a model, which still allows for competiveness in the individual sectors. The private sector can also benefit from the results by being able to identify suggested security best practices for critical infrastructure protection using this model. The public sector will benefit from this study by becoming aware of any shortcomings of the public-private partnership model necessary to ensure the security of critical infrastructures needed to run the country. The study could also allow the public sector the ability to work effectively with the private sector in utilizing the existing model or in the creation of a new model.

## Nature of the Study

The usage of an exploratory case study, using interviews, allowed the researcher to obtain data for the development of suggested best practices (Stebbins, 2001). Performing a qualitative analysis with the use of an exploratory case study as the method was appropriate for this study, as this case study approach allowed for candid capturing of data from the study's participants (Yin, 2014). It also added two additional sources of evidence the first being direct observation of the participant and the second being the data collected during the interviews of the participant (2014). This study allowed Company XYZ to have influence in determining how the security frameworks designed using the public-private partnership model aid in identifying suggested security best practices. Company XYZ, from the communications sector, provided the necessary representation to this exploratory case study. The usage of interviews allowed the study to determine how the security frameworks designed using the public-private partnership model aid in the identification of suggested security best practices as well as the appropriateness of the public-private partnership model in protecting Company XYZ's critical infrastructure.

The general population for this study was a representative sample of employees from Company XYZ within the communications sector. The population included a mix of employees at varying levels of responsibility including senior management, all of who are tasked with the goal to implement adequate protections to protect critical infrastructure. The questions in the interviews allowed for a representative sample from Company XYZ and supported the researcher in determining how security frameworks designed using the public-private partnership model aid in identifying suggested security best practices for Company XYZ's critical infrastructure. As this was a qualitative exploratory case study, unlike a quantitative case study, the study did not perform an assessment on variables. The employees within Company XYZ were the study's sample population; the selections from this population determined how the security frameworks designed using the public-private partnership model aid in the identification of suggested security best practices in protecting Company XYZ's critical infrastructure.

The appropriateness and rationale behind the usage of this population is easily seen when looking at the structure and design of the National Infrastructure Protection Plan. The National Infrastructure Protection Plan is a living document as the threats to critical infrastructure are in a constant state of flux and the partners of the critical infrastructure sectors are fighting the battle on the front lines daily. These partners are best suited to determine how the security frameworks designed using the public-private partnership model aid in the identification of suggested security best practices (NIPP, 2013).

### Research Questions and Hypotheses

This study utilized an exploratory case study, using interviews, completed by employees from within Company XYZ. It utilized interviews with questions geared towards determining how the security frameworks designed using the public-private partnership model aid in the identification of suggested security best practices. The use of an exploratory case study, using interviews, allowed the researcher to explore a problem where the data does not completely define it (Stebbins, 2001). The research questions were qualitatively orientated for this study. The research questions allowed the researcher to best define, through the eyes of Company XYZ's employees, whether or not the security frameworks designed using the public-private partnership model aid in allowing their organization to adequately create suggested security best practices to protect Company XYZ's critical infrastructure.

**Research Question**

The research question for this study concerned the best way to protect critical infrastructure in the United States. To do this there must be an element of collaboration between the public and private sector in identifying suggested security best practices. The collaboration must then ensure there is full protection of the critical resources from both outside and inside attacks. The research question this study addressed, "Is the lack of identifying suggested security best practices to protect critical infrastructure from cyberattacks adequately addressed by utilizing the public-private partnership model and frameworks designed using that model?"

**Theoretical Framework**

The theoretical framework for this study centered on determining how the security frameworks designed using the public-private partnership model aid in identifying suggested security best practices for critical infrastructure protection at Company XYZ. While determining, how the security frameworks designed using the public-private partnership model will aid in identifying suggested security best practices for a telecommunication provider's critical infrastructures the question of the actual importance of the partnership model entered into the discussion. Before the public-private partnership model's use for critical infrastructure protection, the public-private partnership model supplemented and supported department of transportation projects within local and government municipalities.

One of the first frameworks designed using the public-private partnership model was the public-private partnership (P3) equilibrium framework. Michael Garvin created the P3 Equilibrium Framework in 2007 and then modified the framework with Doran Bosso in 2008 to nurture the development of the partnership model as it related to long-term contractual arrangements between municipalities and private construction firms. The consensus was to use public-private partnership arrangements only for infrastructure improvements and service deliveries for department of transportation projects (Garvin and Bosso, 2008). This was with the understanding the public-private partnership delivered value and quality to the municipality (2008).

Designed in 2007 by Michael Garvin the P3 Equilibrium Framework was to assess and promote a structure around the thought process of the project (Garvin, 2012). To do this the P3 Equilibrium Framework needed to establish itself across four key environments: state, society, industry, and market (2012). The center of the equilibrium framework called the range of balance is where these four environments converge. The range of balance between these environments is what the project's success depended on (2012).

Another framework that could be adapted to critical infrastructure protection is the Cyber Terrorism Conceptual Framework created by Rabiah Ahmad and Zahri Yunos in 2012. Ahmad and Yunos stated in 2012 the framework was necessary because of the convergence of both the virtual and physical world. The definition of cyber terrorism is the unlawful attack against computers, networks, stored information, and then using the attack to intimidate or coerce a government, business, or person (Ahmad & Yunos, 2012b). The impact to targeted critical infrastructure by cyber terrorism is to cause fear to anyone in the individual sectors as these attacks can cause violence, death, and destruction (2012b). It is with this definition the framework gains a necessary discussion into what framework is the best to protect critical infrastructure.

While both of these frameworks could be adapted easily for critical infrastructure protection, it is both President Barak Obama's Presidential Policy Directive (PPD) – 21 on Critical Infrastructure Security and Resilience and Executive Order (EO) 13636 Improving Critical Infrastructure Cybersecurity in 2013, which paved the path for the creation of a new cybersecurity framework. The path these orders paved allows for the utilization of the public-private partnership model by determining if the security frameworks designed using the model can aid in identifying suggested security best practices. These Presidential directives also tasked the Department of Homeland Security's Planning and Evaluation Working Group Integrated Task Force with deliverables important to this study. The Planning and Evaluation Working Group Integrated Task Force was required to deliver was an evaluation of the current public-private partnership model ability to aid in designing security frameworks and evaluating the partnership model for its functionality surrounding physical and cybersecurity (Integration Task Force Overview, 2013).

It was on February 12, 2014, a new framework was released to the public and is becoming the recommended public-private partnership standard for critical infrastructure protection in the United States (NIST, 2013). The new Framework for Improving Critical Infrastructure Cybersecurity is now available to all infrastructure sectors and is available on the National Institute of Standards and Technology's website (www.nist.gov/cyberframework/index.cfm). This new framework is voluntary but the public and private sector are actively choosing to use it to protect critical infrastructure and this framework is considered a "living" document (Framework for Improving Critical Infrastructure, 2014). The document will continue to evolve with feedback from both the private and public sector partners (2014).

The new framework will enable sector partners to apply suggested best practices and use the principles of risk management to improve the security and resilience of the critical infrastructure it protects (2014). It will continually push for collaboration between sector partners (public-private partnership) to establish new risk-based standards (Trope and Humes, 2013). The framework focuses on using business drivers to guide individual and group cybersecurity activities and it will consider cybersecurity risk as part of an organization's overall risk management program (Framework for Improving Critical Infrastructure, 2014). The effective usage of this new framework will allow sector partners to respond and react more quickly to threats and limit those threat's potential effects to their services and enterprise (Trope and Humes, 2013). This framework will become a focus of this study and will aid in the determination if it is indeed the right model (private-public partnership) and framework to aid in the identification of suggested security best practices for the protection of critical infrastructure for the United States.

**Definition of Terms**

*Critical Infrastructure* – is any infrastructure within the United States that is critical to the function of the society and its economy (NIPP, 2010). It is typically comprised of an interconnected set of systems and assets, physical and virtual, which is critical to the daily needs of the population (Alcaraz & Zeadally, 2013). These needs are necessary for the health and welfare of the population and include water, electricity, communications, and thirteen other critical sectors (NIPP, 2010).

*Critical Infrastructure Protection* –relates to the preparedness and response to serious incidents upon critical infrastructures within the nation (NIPP, 2010).

*DHS* – Department of Homeland Security is the agency tasked with the protections around critical infrastructure for the United States.

*EO – Executive Order 13636 – Improving Critical Infrastructure Cybersecurity* – is a policy presented by President Barak Obama to strengthen critical infrastructure protection for the United States (EO-13636).

*FCC – Federal Communications Commission* – is the federal agency tasked with providing varying degrees of oversight and leadership to communications bodies within the United States.

*HSPD-7 – Homeland Security Presidential Directive 7* – is the directive designed to ensure adequate protection around the sixteen most critical infrastructures within the United States (HSPD-7).

*NIPP – National Infrastructure Protection Plan* – is the plan drafted by the Department of Homeland Security and its partners as a guide to critical infrastructure protection (NIPP, 2010).

*NIST – National Institute of Standards and Technology* – is one of the Federal Agencies heading up the task to building President Obama's Cybersecurity Framework necessary for the protection of the Nation's critical infrastructure.

*PPD – Presidential Policy Directive– 21 on Critical Infrastructure Security and Resilience* – is an additional order from the Office of President Barak Obama to strengthen and add resiliency to critical infrastructure in the United States (PPD-21).

*PPP or P3 – Public-Private Partnership Model* – is a model used by the Department of Homeland Security allowing government (i.e. public) agencies and those in the private sector to work together to reach a common goal (Garvin, 2012).

*PSTN –Public Switched Telephone Network* – includes items such as telephone lines, cables, fiber optics, and satellite communications connected in a worldwide network (NIPP, 2010).

*Telecommunications Act of 1996* – this was the first significant change to telecommunications law since 1936 and included laws centered on cable and band spectrums for cellular/mobile networks (NIPP, 2010).

### Assumptions

There were a few basic assumptions made within this exploratory case study. The assumptions were the following:

a) The researcher will understand the responses provided by the Company XYZ's employees and the researcher will accurately analyze the employee's responses in relation to the research question.

b) Company XYZ's employees will demonstrate integrity, sincerity, and truthfulness in their responses during the interview.

c) The literature review conducted by the researcher in support of this study will be sufficient to represent the intentions and purpose of the study correctly.

An essential assumption also exists that an exploratory case study will contain a mixture of questions providing the breadth and depth required for the relevant analysis of the findings (Blair, Czaja and Blair, 2014). Within this framework, the assumption was the researcher's knowledge allowed for a necessary understanding of the major factors and was satisfactory to minimize any effects of bias within the results. To lessen any inherent risks associated with these assumptions, the researcher attempted to ensure Company XYZ's employees, who have been selected, can participate in the research study. The researcher obtained all responses in a truthful and honest manner, reflecting only Company XYZ's employees understanding, and point of view. The researcher remained impartial and detached from the interview to ensure no bias or prejudice was introduced in the findings. The questions were included to ensure objectivity of Company XYZ employee's responses and allow the experience to emerge (Creswell, 2012).

## Scope

The scope of this project was to conduct interviews with fifteen subject matter experts within Company XYZ listed as a Department of Homeland Security critical infrastructure. These subject matter experts provided the necessary feedback to the researcher to determine if the participants have an understanding of the public-private partnership model and critical infrastructure. The central part of the study focused on determining how security frameworks designed using the public-private partnership model aid in the identification of suggested security best practices to protect critical infrastructure for Company XYZ in the United States. The data obtained through this study could be easily generalized across the other remain critical infrastructures as all sectors have a need to identify suggested security best practice to protect the respective sector. This generalizability of the study's findings allows for additional research opportunities as it relates to critical infrastructure protection in the United States.

## Limitations

This study was limited by the fact a small number of employees from Company XYZ will be utilized. Only the selected employees from Company XYZ were necessary for the completion of this study. An additional limitation presented within this study was the lack of influence from any regulatory agencies. While regulatory agencies are present within the Communications Sector, the study did not look at those influences. This study was limited as there was little to no scholarly research on how one can determine how security frameworks designed using the public-private partnership model aid in identifying suggested security best practices for critical infrastructure protection of telecommunication providers. This allows for some variance in the outcome of the study but does limit the depth and breadth of data found on the topic.

## Delimitations

The delimitations for this study allowed the researcher to focus the study on looking solely at the research question at hand. The first delimitation was that the researcher was only looking at a single critical infrastructure partner using the public-private partnership model. This study was solely looking at the National Infrastructure Protection Plan created by the Department of Homeland Security for critical infrastructure protection. Another delimitation for this study reflects the literature chosen for review centering on determining how security frameworks designed using the public-private partnership model aid in identifying suggested security best practices for critical infrastructure protection. Even though the public-private partnership model is widely used for other studies and processes, for the purposes of this study the researcher will facilitate the public-private partnership model usage for protecting critical infrastructure for Company XYZ. A final delimitation on this study was the population selected to question in regards to determining how security frameworks designed using the public-private partnership model aid in suggested security best practice identification. The population was across one telecommunications provider, Company XYZ, within the communication sector to get a representative sample.

## Summary

Chapter 1 allowed the researcher to present the purpose and problem of this study. The specific problem was private and public sector partners lack standardized security best practices to protect critical infrastructure from cyberattack. The study determined how security frameworks designed using the public-private partnership model aid in identifying suggested security best practices and determined if there was a lack of adequate collaboration. The study used an exploratory case study, using interviews, allowing members from within Company XYZ to have an adequate voice in determining how security frameworks designed using the public-private partnership model aid in the identification of suggested security best practices.

The study was based on an exploratory case methodology, allowing for qualitative analysis using a question and answer format. Such a methodology was appropriate because although there was significant academic research relating to critical infrastructure in general, little research has been conducted so far on determining how security frameworks designed using the public-private partnership model aid in identifying suggested security best practices. The use of an exploratory case study, using interviews, allowed the researcher to explore a problem the data does not completely define (Stebbins, 2001).

The uniqueness of this study lies in the current lack of academic research on the security frameworks designed using the partnership model. Businesses and private entities within the communications sector are in competition on a daily basis and it seems very unlikely these businesses would be willing to freely share the suggested security best practices designed by the brand they represent. As this sharing of confidential and proprietary information could allow a competitor to have an unfair advantage against the other in the marketplace. It is this research methodology and uniqueness of the study materials that allowed the researcher to determine how security frameworks designed using the public-private partnership model aid in identifying suggested security best practices within Company XYZ. As the study moves into Chapter 2, the Literature Review, the literature surrounding the public-private partnership model and its usage in critical infrastructure protection was looked at so a foundation can be built upon the possibility of the Department of Homeland Security in using this partnership model as their method of choice for the National Infrastructure Protection Plan.

# CHAPTER 2: REVIEW OF THE LITERATURE

The interaction, and interdependencies of the public-private partnership model and the model's relationship with identifying suggested security best practices for critical infrastructure protection was examined in this review. The protection of those entities within the communications sector, one of the Department of Homeland Security's sixteen critical infrastructure sectors will also be investigated. The review began with an overview of the public-private partnership model from its historical beginnings and continuing through its use in the Department of Homeland Security's plans for critical infrastructure protections (NIPP Communications Sector Overview). This transition in the review will focus on the Homeland Security Presidential Directive 7 (HSPD-7). The HSPD-7 directive designed the protection around the sixteen most critical infrastructures within the United States. The history of the communications sector was looked at in detail to see how it relates to the National Infrastructure Protection Plan.

The literature review reveals the lack of scholarly research in regards to determining how security frameworks designed using the public-private partnership model aid in the identification of suggested security best practices for critical infrastructure protection. It looked at how private industries that compete in common workspaces can be effective in providing the necessary critical control updates to the government counterparts to ensure a solid and seamless cooperation between them. This cooperation is necessary for a public-private partnership to succeed. All scholarly research addressing the challenges for critical infrastructure protection was looked at. It will ensure a competitive marketplace between private entities continues while still allowing for adequate collaborating for the National Infrastructure Protection Plan to work. Finally, the review looked at ways to determine how security frameworks designed using the public-private partnership model aid in identifying suggested security best practices to protect critical infrastructure.

## Title Searches, Articles, Research Documents and Journals

The literature obtained for this study came from searches of the following databases: EBSCOhost, ProQuest, ABI/INFORM, ACM Digital Library, IEEE Computer Society Digital Library, SAGE Journals and Security Management Practices. While searching though the numerous available databases, the most used keywords were as follows: *public-private, partnership, public-private partnership, critical infrastructure, critical infrastructure protection, data security, Internet protection, DHS, cybersecurity policy, executive order, presidential policy directive (PPD), Cybersecurity Framework, Equilibrium Model, NIPP, effectiveness, and communications sector.* Appendix A contains the Key Literature Review Search Terms and Appendix B contains the Literature Search used for this study.

## The Need for Critical Infrastructure Protection

The need for protection of critical infrastructures has been a major priority of the United States government. Daily, the news headlines are discussing the newest malware or recent cyber-attacks. Brechbuhl, Bruce, Dynes, and Johnson (2010) mentioned in a networked world there is no safe haven and if you are on the network then you are equally vulnerable to cyberattack. As examples, Glennon (2012) cites the 2009 breach of Google's email system and hackers breaking into the US national electric grid. The attacks on Estonia's critical systems, meanwhile, as well as cyber-attacks connected with Russia's invasion of Georgia show how linked the entire world has become (Glennon,

2012). Nations are concerned not only about the tools of cyber warfare but also about the use of these tools by terrorist organizations (Goel, 2011). Cyber-attacks are becoming more frequent and the payloads more sophisticated and malicious causing larger outages and downtimes (Tofan, Andrei and Dinca, 2012). Since the Internet has no political or geographic boundaries, countries are going to have to work together and share cyber security responsibilities (Brechbuhl et al, 2010). Each country and private sector member also becomes a responsible stakeholder under the public-private partnership model; this is what the United States National Infrastructure Protection Plan was built on (2010).

The Internet has become a necessity in every country in the developed and developing world and securing the Internet has become a national priority (Tofan, Andrei and Dinca, 2012). Critical infrastructure protection is currently seen as an element of national security and in most parts of the world nations are trying to determine the best ways to protect it (Cavelty and Suter, 2009). Another important step in protecting the critical infrastructure is awareness because an increase in awareness of risk can allow for better cybersecurity decisions by sector leaders (Brechbuhl et al, 2010). However, the main point and decision of the Department of Homeland Security is to select the public-private partnership model which is a collaborative effort by the partners allowing for more effective cybersecurity policy and interoperability between policy frameworks (2010).

## History of the Public-Private Partnership Model

A public-private partnership is an agreement between two entities, one being a private sector entity and the other a public or government agency allowing for a combination and collaboration of resources, skills and personnel to develop or in the case of critical infrastructures to protect a technology (Cellucci, 2010). This allows for the joint collaboration of resources, innovation and expertise not present in one collaborate but ample in the other partner (Cavelty and Suter, 2009). It is important to understand "public" in this context does not imply government control; rather, it means the government acts as protector (INSA, 2009). An effective public-private partnership, as it relates to cyber security, should provide an ability to determine both dangerous anomalies and threats (2009).

**Early Days – Colonial Times to World War I**

The public-private partnership model has been considered the most significant trend within the public sector in allowing for adequate collaboration (Garvin, 2012). The history of public-private partnerships in the United States dates back to colonial times. In 1631 John Winthrop Jr., was instrumental in creating the idea of government working with private businesses in the effort to benefit society (Cellucci, 2010). Benjamin Franklin followed suit in 1742 by helping to advance science with the sponsoring of his society, The American Philosophical Society of Philadelphia and the Pennsylvania House of Representatives to the University of Pennsylvania (2010). The Lewis and Clark Expedition was a sponsorship by the government to a private exploratory team created by Meriwether Lewis and William Clark (2010). These public-private partnerships continued on an evolutionary path through work and support during times of need such as the Chicago Fire of 1871 and have continued to evolve as the partnerships have become more critical to the defense of the United States (Busch & Givens, 2012).

During the 1900's, the practice of public-private partnerships continued to grow during World War I, where President Woodrow Wilson established the Council of

National Defense to identify domestic research programs that would benefit the defense of the nation (Cellucci, 2010). Introduced in 1906, the Berlin Treaty addressed an emerging world problem dealing with cyber-commons to head off the first cyber disaster (Rutkowski, 2010). This cyber disaster dealt with the world's new dependence on wireless telegraph and radio communications and was ratified by the following nations: Germany, Argentina, Austria, Hungary, Belgium, Brazil, Bulgaria, Chile, Denmark, Spain, France, Great Britain, Greece, Italy, Japan, Mexico, Monaco, Norway, Netherlands, Persia, Portugal, Romania, Russia, Sweden, Turkey, and Uruguay (International Radiotelegraph Conference – Berlin, 1906). These nations agreed to the Treaties seven main principles: do no harm, identity management, effective information exchange, interoperability, enhance infrastructure resilience and protection, prioritize capabilities for emergencies, and continual international cooperation (Rutkowski, 2010). It was not until 1912 when the United States ratified the 1906 Berlin Treaty, with the support of President Taft, after it finally made its way through the US Congress. It took the sinking of the H.M.S. Titanic in the North Atlantic Ocean to show how necessary the treaty was. The Berlin Treaty was ratified by the US Congress four days after the Titanic's sinking and included additional domestic and international actions created by the United States and other ratifying nations, this was called the London Treaty of 1912 (2010). The lack of responsiveness by the United States towards the treaty was due in part to private industries' insistence the treaty's provisions could impede technology and innovation (2010). There was concern over government involvement in the matters of private industry, as well as a distrust of foreign nations' involvement (2010).

## World War II to Today

During World War II, the public-private partnership model continued to gain momentum as the chairperson of the President's Scientific Research Board, John Steelman, created a report entitled "Science and Public Policy". This report was presented to President Harry S. Truman and contained five recommendations on how the Federal Government could benefit from scientific research with the aid of the private sector (Cellucci, 2010). These recommendations were as follows:

1. Need for Basic Research

2. Prosperity

3. International Progress

4. Increase Cost of Discovery

5. National Security

These recommendations were set as the basis for the public-private partnership model. This basic public-private partnership model continued taking shape during the Cold War where it was used to aid the moon landing program under President John F. Kennedy, President Richard M. Nixon's war on cancer and President Jimmy Carter's programs to develop renewable energy sources (2010).

As computer systems integrate into businesses and within the public and private infrastructure, the growing dependency on the most critical of those infrastructures comes under the microscope (Stephan, 2006). These critical infrastructures could contain points of vulnerability, which if used maliciously or unintentionally could cripple the United States as well as other developed countries (2006). The vulnerabilities range from relatively mild disruptions of a company's e-mail or online ordering system to catastrophic attacks on key infrastructure, resulting in destruction of equipment and loss of life. Targets such as oil refineries, electric grids, and water supply systems could potentially be targeted (2006). According to Stephan (2006), these computer systems extend across a line from the public sector to the private sector with no discernable boundaries.

Baines and Chiarelott (2010) noted declining revenues from organizations in both the public and private sector have made it necessary to build a new partnership. Cavelty and Suter (2009) stated the public-private partnership model has been seen as the potential savior to critical infrastructure protection. This is primarily because the cooperation between the government and private sector allows for the mixing of talent and finance (Cavelty and Suter, 2009). Due to this necessity, the Department of Homeland Security chose to implement a unified protective environment using the public-private partnership model as its cornerstone when drafting the National Infrastructure Protection Plan (Stephan, 2006). These new partnerships have allowed public sector organizations to utilize lower prices provided by gaining access to the assets of private organizations (Baines & Chiarelott, 2010). Meidute and Paliulis (2011) identified a principle driver in utilizing a public-private partnership is due to the efficiency of performing the necessary functions not typically possessed by the public sector. To be successful the public-private partnership needs to coordinate the interests of all the sector partners, spread and manage the risk, control the performance and manage the overall partnership (Meidute & Paliulis, 2011). However, the key differentiator of the public-private partnerships successfulness is the effectiveness of the partners to meet the overall goal of the project (2011).

**Frameworks Used with the Public-Private Partnership Model**

This study evaluated three cybersecurity frameworks that have been designed for critical infrastructure protection utilizing the public-private partnership model. This discussion looked at the design, its primary usage, and how it will benefit a critical infrastructure in protecting the partner's infrastructure. The study looked first at the P3 Equilibrium Framework designed in 2007 by Michael J. Garvin and used primarily within the transportation infrastructure projects. The second framework was the Cyber Terrorism Conceptual Framework designed in 2012 by Rabiah Ahmad and Zahri Yunos to defend critical infrastructure from terrorist attacks. The final framework looked at in this study is the Framework for Improving Critical Infrastructure which was designed in 2013-2014 as a collaboration of public and private partners surrounding President Barrack Obama's call for better cybersecurity defense of critical infrastructure. This final framework was looked at in more depth as it was built exclusively by a public-private partnership to protect critical infrastructure in the United States.

**P3 Equilibrium Framework**

The first framework created by Michael Garvin in 2007 for usage around the public-private partnership model surrounding Department of Transportation projects (Garvin & Bosso, 2008). Garvin (2010) added the usage of the public-private partnership model in the transportation sector came primarily out of the necessity created by economic hardships and it allowed for a stimulus to help rebound the economy. The framework he created, the P3 Equilibrium Framework, looks at the public-private partnership model to determine the models overall effectiveness. The objective of a public-private partnership under this framework is to nurture the development of the partnership model and sustain its existence (Garvin & Bosso, 2008). The framework seeks to determine the effectiveness of the public-partnership model based on collective performance of the project(s) and the project relationship to its strategy or policy for the management and development to the infrastructure (2008).

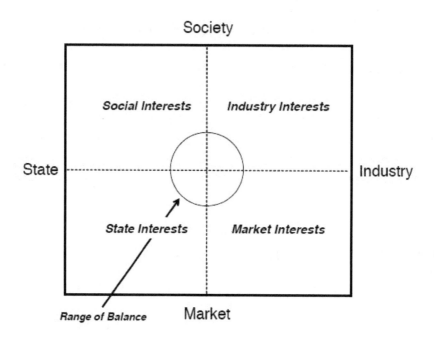

*Figure 1.* The P3 Equilibrium Framework. Adapted from "Are Public–Private partnerships effective infrastructure development strategies?" by M. J. Garvin, 2012, Paper presented at the *CME 25: Conference Construction Management and Economics: Past, Present and Future: 16th-18th July 2007*, University of Reading, England. 357.

In Figure 1, the P3 Equilibrium Framework looks at four areas (state, society, industry and market) divided into four quadrants with the center of these quadrants making up the range of balance (Garvin, 2012). The state is the governing body, society is the citizens, industry is made up the organizations providing the service, and the market is the financial system (2012). Garvin (2012) stated there were limitations to this framework as it provided a perspective on the necessary research but lacked the tools for measurement. The framework bases the effectiveness of the public-private partnership model on the quality of the service provided, price, and cost of the service, availability, level of environmental impacts and the distribution of social benefits (Garvin & Bosso, 2008). This framework puts together a general perspective of the how to measure the effectiveness of the public-private partnership model however even Garvin and Bosso (2008) agree no tools are actually provided to determine the necessary measurements of the public-private partnership's effectiveness.

**Cyber Terrorism Conceptual Framework**

The second framework is the creation of Rabiah Ahmad and Zahri Yunos (2012b) called the Cyber Terrorism Conceptual Framework. The design of this framework came out of the necessity of a framework to defend against cyber terrorism attacks to critical infrastructure (Ahmad & Yunos, 2012b). Cyber terrorism can have a critical impact on infrastructure by causing fear, violence, death, and destruction of those critical infrastructures (2012b). This framework describes cyberterrorism as politically motivated, fear causing attacks using cyber, attacks against critical infrastructure, and a disruption of services or for a monetary gain (2012b).

32

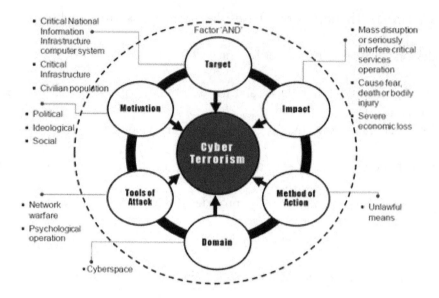

*Figure 2.* The Cyber Terrorism Conceptual Framework. Adapted from "Perception on cyberterrorism: A focus group discussion approach," R. Ahmad, Z. Yunos, S. Sahib, & M. Yusoff, 2012, *Journal of Information Security, 3*(3), 231-237.

Rabiah Ahmad, Zahri Yunos, Shahrin Sahib, and Mariana Yusoff (2012) built this framework (Figure 2) for critical infrastructure protection from cyber terrorist attacks by using focus groups to gain a better understanding of key objectives and gain the views and perceptions of the sector members. This research coupled with the interviews conducted by Ahmad and Yunos (2012) were looking for common patterns. This framework is still in the design phase but could be adapted to the frameworks studied for public-private partnerships and as such is relevant to discuss in this research.

**Framework for Improving Critical Infrastructure Cybersecurity**

INSA (2009) found there were three unique items specific to the usage of the public-private partnership models usage for critical infrastructure protection. These three items brought about the creation of the third model currently being developed and rolled out to the critical infrastructure sector. According to INSA (2009) these items were:

1) Issues surrounding who owns what in cyber space

2) Members may operate under established regulatory requirements from state, federal or international organizations

3) The time scale surrounding cyber initiatives (development, responses) are shorter than with other usages of the public-private partnership model

These unique factors made all current public-private partnership models ineffective for critical infrastructure protection (INSA, 2009). It was in May 2011 major cybersecurity legislation was proposed (Schmidt, 2011). It was out of this new legislation the next framework's design was created (2011).

| Function Unique Identifier | Function | Category Unique Identifier | Category |
|---|---|---|---|
| ID | Identify | ID.AM | Asset Management |
| | | ID.BE | Business Environment |
| | | ID.GV | Governance |
| | | ID.RA | Risk Assessment |
| | | ID.RM | Risk Management Strategy |
| PR | Protect | PR.AC | Access Control |
| | | PR.AT | Awareness and Training |
| | | PR.DS | Data Security |
| | | PR.IP | Information Protection Processes and Procedures |
| | | PR.MA | Maintenance |
| | | PR.PT | Protective Technology |
| DE | Detect | DE.AE | Anomalies and Events |
| | | DE.CM | Security Continuous Monitoring |
| | | DE.DP | Detection Processes |
| RS | Respond | RS.RP | Response Planning |
| | | RS.CO | Communications |
| | | RS.AN | Analysis |
| | | RS.MI | Mitigation |
| | | RS.IM | Improvements |
| RC | Recover | RC.RP | Recovery Planning |
| | | RC.IM | Improvements |
| | | RC.CO | Communications |

*Figure 3.* Framework for Improving Critical Infrastructure Cybersecurity. Adapted from "Framework for Improving Critical Infrastructure Cybersecurity," by National Institute of Standards and Technology, 2014.

This new framework is the Framework for Improving Critical Infrastructure Cybersecurity; the National Institute of Standards and Technology released this new framework on February 12, 2014. This framework came out of Executive Order 13636 President Barack Obama tasked both the Federal (public) and private sector partners to create (NIST, 2014). It uses business drivers to guide an organization's cybersecurity initiatives and calculates cyber risk into the overall management process (2014). To accomplish this, the new framework aligns the organization's key businesses requirements to the cybersecurity initiatives the organization is striving to obtain (2014).

The ultimate purpose of this new framework is to allow the sector partners to align the organizations to security best practices and increase the resilience against attack

(2014). The Framework for Improving Critical Infrastructure is the focus of this research to determine the overall effectiveness to protecting critical infrastructure. The growing importance within the nation on critical infrastructure and the seriousness of the threats being handled almost daily brought about these necessary changes (Daniel, 2013). The challenge to the framework's success is incentives to support the frameworks adoption (Daniel, 2013). These incentives will focus on cybersecurity insurance, grants, process, liability limitation, streamlining of regulations and research incentives (2013).

**History of the National Infrastructure Protection Plan**

With America's growing demand and reliance on critical infrastructure such as water, communications, and electricity so is, the demand placed upon the Federal government to protect critical infrastructure from attack. The infrastructure primary to the communications sector is the Internet. The Internet is necessary for one to have a functioning ability in commerce, government, and personal and most importantly for national security (INSA, 2009). INSA (2009) determined nearly all facets of the modern world rely on the Internet and it is a superhighway for malicious individuals to move about freely and undetected. President Bill Clinton determined the Internet should be considered a critical infrastructure (Parsons & Safdar, 2011). The former Cybersecurity Coordinator for the White House, Howard Schmidt, stated during an interview that Presidential Decision Directive (PPD) 63, issued by President Bill Clinton in 1998, reflected the growing concern over critical infrastructure protection (Parsons and Safdar, 2011). PPD 63 was created to address the role of the private sector and public sector (Parsons and Safdar, 2011). The directive also requested the private sector voluntarily organize to address critical infrastructure protection and it created councils for the specific sectors to coordinate partners within their unique niches (2011).

**Necessity of the National Infrastructure Protection Plan**

Critical infrastructure affects all citizens (Ridley, 2011). These critical infrastructures are systems and sets interconnect both physically and virtually and are necessary to support the daily activities and functions of citizens (Alcaraz & Zeadally, 2013). This includes the infrastructure that supplies the energy (electric, gas, and oil), Internet services, water, and banking. Ridley (2011) stated interruptions of these essential services could have considerable consequences. A critical failure of one or more of the critical infrastructures can cause a cascading effect ultimately causing not just a single disruption but could ultimately create multiple (Caldeira, et al., 2011). This cascading effect can best be described by the electric grid, which is comprised of numerous providers interconnected to one another. If one of these providers goes down it could put extra strain on the system in another area causing the system to go down and this cascade of effects can continue until all of the providers go down and the country is in total darkness and chaos (2011).

The issue arose early where in the 1990's government looked to the private sector to provide infrastructure that currently needs protection (Ridley, 2011). Infrastructures such as electric, water, gas, oil, and Internet technologies are considered the most critical. The Internet is not secure, it has well-documented issues, and it is widely known and understood these issues open up vulnerabilities (Hall, 2012). These vulnerabilities can cause major service disruptions (Hall, 2012). Hall's reasoning for these statements is because the Internet is comprised of interconnected networks; this is in his words is the technologies greatest vulnerability (2012).

This vulnerability of the Internet comes into play because of the overall design of it. Adding security to the Internet causes tradeoffs in relation to convenience; the Internet was meant to be flexible and easy to use (Li & Unger, 1995). These convenience elements of openness, flexibility, ease of access, cooperation between users, and interdependencies causes the Internet to be unsecure (1995). This adds risk to the networks attached to the Internet as there are more points of attack; the physical perimeter has extended into almost every business and home, and the amount of services offered off these networks (1995). It is these inherited vulnerabilities in the Internet that partners in critical infrastructure must take the time to adequately protect critical infrastructure (1995).

One of the main issues at hand is critical infrastructure is dependent on multiple providers interconnected systems as well as the legacy equipment between those providers (Bessani et al, 2008). The other factor besides the interdependence between providers is these systems were never designed with security in mind (2008). Ultimately these older systems now connected to the Internet have inadequate security to protect it from malicious actors (2008). These systems were designed before the necessity of interconnecting systems and linking everything back to the Internet. The security they employed was based on obscurity and these controllers were designed with weak security standards that are easy to break today (2008). The Internet these controllers are linked to and powered by the critical electric grid allows for compromises because there are no physical boundaries, making it easy to exploit these vulnerabilities from anywhere in the world (Avina, 2011). The Internet is a complex interconnected spider web of digital and information infrastructures that provides critical support to communications and national security (Maughan, 2010). No single Federal agency or private organization owns the Internet, however; the protection of the Internet is a national and global challenge, which requires cooperation across both the private and public sector (2010).

Hall (2012) reiterates the necessity of cooperation in critical infrastructure protection, which is the greatest strength of the Internet. Multiple private partners protect the Internet and these private partners' resources are what aid in its protection. Such cooperation is necessary because both sectors are completely dependent of one another but share equally the responsibility to protect critical infrastructure (Maughan, 2010). The issue at hand is security protections around critical infrastructure are expensive and the threat landscape is ever changing, hence the necessity of the private sector to look for additional sources of funding (2010). Research and development costs could be offset if collaboration between the private and the public sector was enhanced as it could allow for more innovation and protective measures to be created (2010). To meet this challenge, the Federal government elected to reach out to the owners of these critical infrastructures in an effort to build a risk management solution for private industries to better assess risk, prioritize needs and to execute the necessary protective measures (Stephan, 2006). Avina (2011) spoke about the necessity of having strong sustainable partnerships that government partners needed to ensure requests were determined in a way to allow for clear and measurable results.

## Creation of the Department of Homeland Security

The creation of the Department of Homeland Security allowed the government to build the necessary partnerships with the private sector to identify critical infrastructures (Parsons and Safdar, 2011). It was in 2002 the Department of Homeland Security created partnerships of equals to allow for the development of technology, standards and practices ensuring the Department of Homeland Security would not be dictating to the private sector what it felt were necessary for cyber security (Clinton, 2011). The department set out on this journey to determine what they needed to do to build this public-private partnership. The issue the department needed to address first was the fact the traditional threat models did not hold and historical indicators to predict future attacks on critical infrastructure protection could not be used (Stephan, 2006).

According to Stephan (2006), the main reason surrounding the failure of traditional threat models was the growing interdependencies on critical systems allowed for devastating attacks on infrastructure. The growing threat of cyber-attacks and intrusions has become one of the most serious issues to national security (George, 2011). To address this, the Department of Homeland Security sought to get a better understanding of what the cyber threats were to these critical infrastructures (Stephan, 2006). As George (2011) points out, critical infrastructure partners face a threat landscape evolving at a pace that does not allow them to keep up. To address this dilemma, the Department of Homeland Security created a new risk approach called the National Infrastructure Protection Plan. This plan details how the partners will work to identify, prioritize, and conduct risk assessments across the critical infrastructure areas (Stephan, 2006). The sixteen areas covered by the National Infrastructure Protection Plan are:

Chemical, Commercial Facilities, Critical Manufacturing, Dams, Defense Industry, Emergency Services, Energy, Financial, Food and Agriculture, Government Facilities, Healthcare and Public Health, Information Technology, Nuclear, Transportation, Water and the focus of this research Communications (United States Department of Homeland Security, 2014).

**Overview of the National Infrastructure Protection Plan**

The Department of Homeland Security set out to build the underlying structure of this risk management based solution. It utilized the public-private partnership model to allow security partners from each sector to work side by side to produce a comprehensive, systematic, and rationalized assessment to reduce risk to the infrastructure base (Stephan, 2006). Risk is the measure of likelihood an undesirable consequence will happen in the future and involves additional metrics around impact to the overall organization (Podbregar and Podbregar, 2012). The operational risk to a critical system is measured by the level of the threat to the system times the degree of the vulnerability (Bessani et al, 2008). Risk management according to Podbregar and Podbregar (2012) is the acts of controlling risk by identifying it, assessing it, managing it, and controlling it. By accomplishing these tasks, risk management can provide an assurance of achieving an organization's objectives by being proactive instead of reactive (Podbregar and Podbregar, 2012).

**Risk Management and the National Infrastructure Protection Plan**

The National Infrastructure Protection Plan also includes cross sector capabilities, which help to lay the cornerstone of the protection plan (Stephan, 2006). This cornerstone is the risk management framework, which set up the processes used to combine consequences, vulnerabilities, and threat information; it was the combination of these three elements, used to assess the risks to the infrastructure(s) (2006). The National Infrastructure Protection Plan is a risk management framework comprised of six main activities (2006).

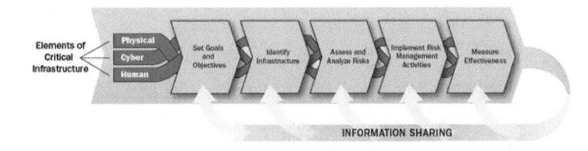

*Figure 4.* Critical Infrastructure Risk Management Framework. Adapted from "National Infrastructure Protection Plan," by United States Department of Homeland Security, 2013.

It is these six risk management activities that have been devised to address the three basic factors of risk (consequences, vulnerabilities of systems and threat vectors) because once these three elements are combined the activities form the risk to the infrastructure (Stephan, 2006). The six activities are as follows:

1. Set Security Goals

2. Identify the Assets

3. Assess the Risks

4. Prioritize

5. Implement Protective Measures

6. Measure the Effectiveness

These six activities together form an assessment of risks to critical infrastructure and collaboration between the public and private sectors. It is when these entities utilize the process that a seamless integration is possible. Geer (2013) stated risk is a consequence of our own dependency and the goals of risk mitigation are no longer intrusion prevention but intrusion tolerance. Working together cyber risk management can reduce the threat landscape to a manageable level to reduce risk to the Nation's most critical infrastructures (Stephan, 2006). Adequate collaboration is necessary to create common tools to strengthen cybersecurity capabilities around an effective risk management framework (Schmidt, 2012).

**Collaboration on the National Infrastructure Protection Plan**

It is with this close collaboration with the Department of Homeland Security that critical infrastructure organizations will be able to overhaul the approaches to counter cyber-attacks and prevent the loss of critical data, disclosure of data or destruction of data (George, 2011). To overhaul the approaches the organizations need to look at controls designed to prevent errors and include procedures for correcting errors if they should arise (Podbregar and Podbregar, 2012). The necessity of the National Infrastructure Protection Plan, however, is demonstrated by the fact most of today's critical infrastructures require minimal user interaction, thus putting more emphasis on creating a seamless plan to effectively manage risk (Alcaraz & Lopez, 2013). The National Infrastructure Protection Plan is a critical piece necessary to build a solid framework around critical infrastructure protections but it needs to build upon solid cybersecurity principles.

Katzan (2011) stated there are five cybersecurity principles necessary for a national policy. Katzan stated in his paper in 2011 the following five principles are necessary:

- Leadership needs to come from the top down

- The proper capacities are necessary for a digital nation

- Sharing of cybersecurity responsibilities across both private and public organizations

- Effective information sharing and incident response efforts

- Innovation is necessary for future growth

These principles take center stage in the new Framework for Improving Critical Infrastructure Cybersecurity (NIST, 2014). This new framework came out of a White House Executive Order and was backed by the efforts to create a seamless national backbone for digital capacity (DHS Executive Order 13636, 2013). The framework utilizes the public-private partnership model to share responsibilities across sector partners, exchanging information critical for protection and incident response and creating future innovation (Grossman, 2012). This information sharing will come not just from the sharing between partners but with the government as it leader (Daniel, 2014). It also tasks the government with responsibilities to assess the existing regulatory environment and to identify where insufficiencies are located (Daniel, 2014). However, the purpose of this framework was still to maintain a voluntary program (2014).

**The Communications Sector**

The communications sector of the National Infrastructure Protection Plan looks to enhance the nation's infrastructure protection utilizing a partnership through both public and private sector partners (NIPP, 2010). The public sector supports individual parts of the plan by executing, commanding, controlling and coordinating; by providing national, economic and homeland security; and by ensuring the public's health and safety (2010). The private sector is responsible for enhancing the security and protections around critical infrastructure to safeguard physical, cyber, and human assets; the necessary systems and networks to ensuring continuity of operations and enhances shareholder value (2010).

## Wireline and Satellite Communications

The communications sector has evolved over time from wireline communications to systems now rely on a highly competitive industry of interconnected services encompassing wireless, satellite, cable, and broadcast companies offering similar services (NIPP, 2010). To describe the main industries that comprise the communication sector let us begin with the wireline industries. Wireline is those industries consisting of public switched telephone networks or PSTN's, cable networks and enterprise networks (2010). Today these wireline industries are replacing legacy networks with new high speed converged circuit and packet switched networks can transport numerous services (2010). These broadband services consist of voice, data, and video to name a few are the Internet infrastructure of the United States (2010).

Another industry in this sector is wireless, consisting of cellular, paging and radio (2010). This group also is responsible for the communications systems used by law enforcement and public safety systems hence the criticality of this group (2010). Satellite communications is another major industry in this sector; like the wireline industry, it provides services such as data, voice, and video (backbone services) as well as multicast services providing video and data to large audiences (NIPP, 2010). This technology can deliver two-way point-to-point or meshed converged access as well as multicast capabilities (2010). This communications medium uses orbiting space vehicles to transmit data, voice, and video between terrestrial sites (2010).

**Cable and Broadcasting Industry**

The next industry is cable, which is a subset of the wireline industry; however, this category has matured because of the introduction of hybrid fiber coaxial architectures (NIPP, 2010). Hybrid fiber coaxial architecture segments a cable system into numerous parallel distribution networks based on a three-level topology (2010). This hybrid fiber coaxial architecture topology is comprised of a headend, distribution hubs, and fiber nodes (2010). The final industry in this sector is the broadcasting group, which is comprised of the free, over air radio and television services (2010).

**Events that Shaped the Communications Sector**

The communications sector came to be its current form because of two key events. The first was the breakup of AT&T in 1984 and the second was the creation of the Telecommunications Act of 1996 (NIPP, 2010). These two events allowed for de-regulation of key communications companies and the competitive marketplace we currently see today. While the private sector industries own the majority of the critical infrastructure it is the public sector supporting those systems critical to defense, law enforcement and public safety and it is this interdependence that has increased the necessity of upgrades to these critical infrastructures (2010).

**Modernization of the Communications Sector**

With the involvement of these new communications companies' large investments into fiber facilities and modernization of infrastructures to support the Internet and broadband systems has occurred (NIPP, 2010). During this time, traditional public switched telephone networks were evolving into packet based next generation networks. The new technologies have allowed for a convergence of circuit switched networks with broadband Internet protocol (IP) based ones (2010). The Federal Communications Commission (FCC) also began to push for the creation of a national broadband plan to utilize these new high-speed services (2010). All of these rapidly changing advances also opened up these communications systems to multiple vulnerabilities, exploits, and risks. With the convergence of these technologies, many systems are being linked together which allows for his migration of malware and viruses (2010). It also allows threats to propagate from one critical system to another in the case of SCADA systems in the water or electrical sectors (2010).

Due to the rapidly evolving convergence of communications technologies the fundamentals around customer demand and business necessity are changing to better plan, prioritize and deliver content across the medium (2010). The vulnerabilities once faced on the legacy networks has become more challenging with the next generation networks and this is primarily because of the massive numbers of interconnections (2010). To make these issues worse, the number of these interconnects allows for more rapid and far-reaching cyber-attacks (2010). To combat these challenges, the members of the communications sector, aware of these new threats, have been investing into technologies such as incident detection, prevention and mitigation capabilities which has allowed those members to gain better visibility into the infrastructure they are responsible for (NIPP, 2010). This visibility allows the members to have better control in anomaly detection, denial of service attack detection, botnet detection, malware analysis, and research into other areas of concern to the sector (2010).

The Department of Homeland Security's Office of Emergency Communications allows the Department of Homeland Security to continue its mission of critical infrastructure protection. The mission of the Department of Homeland Security is multi-facetted and comprised of five main parts: prevention of terrorism and enhance security; secure and manage the country's borders; enforce immigration laws; ensure resilience to disasters; safeguard and secure cyberspace (United States Department of Homeland Security, 2014). It is thru the Department of Homeland Security's Emergency Communications Office the mission to safeguard and secure cyberspace that all critical infrastructure members are proven to have necessary mechanisms in place (NIPP, 2010). These mechanisms include the ability to share information, the creation of an integrated warning system to alert all levels of public and private members and citizens, mobility of communications to meet issues relating to disasters, and use of the Internet as the key resource (2010). The communications sector has four main categories; these categories deal with protection and resilience; response and recovery; awareness and cross-sector coordination between the members (2010). The far-reaching effects of the communications sector coupled with the amount of impact vulnerabilities and attacks can bring against its members highlight the necessity to include this area under the Department of Homeland Security's National Infrastructure Protection Plan. The services provided by this sector's members are fundamental to the country's way of life (NIPP, 2010).

**The Public-Private Partnership and the Communications Sector**

Within the communication sector, one of the issues that must be addressed when considering the public-private partnership model is the roles and responsibilities of the individual parties. There are differing opinions between the private and public sectors, which center primarily on people, processes, and technology (Garcia, 2006). There needs to be vigilance of the people to maintain the processes, the processes need to be designed properly and enforced and multiple layers of technology need to be utilized to deter threats (2006). These differing opinions about efforts to protect critical infrastructures have created a lack of security within our information technology dependency (2006). Private sector organizations can either become self-regulators to mitigate risks and adapt to the changing threat landscape or wait for the public sector to mandate the necessary protections (2006). With the creation of the new Cybersecurity Framework Model by NIST, the framework was designed to give the public sector a list of best practices to allow the private sector to work on the mitigation of threats within the infrastructure.

Garcia (2006) added the issues with a wait and see approach by the public sector is flawed. This flaw is in part to the fact that private sector organizations truly understand a systems weaknesses and vulnerabilities and they have the available resources to address the issues (Garcia, 2006). To this end, the best way to approach critical infrastructure protection is a collaborative solution minimizing threats and ensuring systems remain protected (2006). The public sector needs to continue funding research and programs to promote cyber security and the private sector needs to utilize resources to incorporate the protections to critical systems (2006). These programs would be like the new NIST Cybersecurity Framework where the public sector put forth the funding to build a new framework with the input coming from the private sector members.

The collaborative effort between the public and private sectors will establish the best practices in infrastructure protection. To allow this to work a system of trust must exist between the sectors and their partners allowing for the effectiveness of the information received from one another else without this trust the information received may not be taken into proper consideration (Caldeira, et al., 2011). It will also be a deterrent to criminal or state-sponsored entities from attacking or engaging in cybercrime (Garcia, 2006). These systems are for the most part controlled and operated by the private sector and are used to deal with risks on a daily basis where the public sector is more focused on the acute crippling attacks to the critical infrastructure (Clinton, 2005).

The partnership however will thrive if the public and private entities address critical points. These critical points address the ability to communicate effectively, adopt a set of best practices recognized across organizations, research core protocols to remove common threat vectors and to address the dependencies on wireless technology and related vulnerabilities (2005). The sectors need to appreciate the unique set of skills each entity brings to the table and address the necessity of research into a solid cyber risk framework (2005). As Busch and Givens (2012) stated, these partnerships allow for enhanced hiring, resource allocations, trust amongst the sector organizations and technological innovation. The private sector has the ability to fill personnel gaps in critical areas of the public sector, has the finances to achieve critical business objectives, and can specialize in more areas (Busch & Givens, 2012). There also needs to be a way to directly address economic and human behavioral aspects surrounding cybersecurity (Daniel, 2014). Incentives could be used but a way to determine using the partnership within the communications sector is needed. These incentives could level the market and increase the costs to malicious actors (2014).

**Challenges of Using Public-Private Partnership within the Communications Sector**

Considering the criticality of the communication sector to the United States, it would seem there would not be an issue with utilizing the public-private partnership model. While the usage of the partnership model on the surface is a good fit, several challenges remain. An issue determined to be a roadblock to the effective implementation of this public-private partnership is a private partner may be resistant to cooperate on a volunteer basis but the cyber threat needs to be adequately addressed (Obama, 2012). Government needs to make cooperation easier, liability protection needs to be addressed, and information sharing (2012).

These private partners would like to have assurances that information would be confidential and partners would not be liable for vulnerabilities (Federal Register, 2013; IT SCC, 2013; McConnell, 2013; Wildman, 2013; Canfield and Ward, 2013; IT SCC, 2013; Rupy and Mayer, 2013; Chessen, Polk, Podey, Symons, and Harvie, 2013; Coffey, Srihari, and Scarpelli, 2013). One other challenge is in the area of clear communications between individual companies. Another is while the government is eager to learn where vulnerabilities reside within the infrastructure it can be an issue to get critical vulnerability information (Ridley, 2011). Ridley (2011) stated this because of the research conducted which showed private partners were reluctant to disclose private information for fear of penalties for exploited vulnerabilities or attacks causing outages of systems or loss of property and/or life. Cavelty and Suter (2009) also discovered five main issues when implementing a public-private partnership model:

1.  The public sector has no monitoring capabilities to determine if the private sectors are adequately protecting critical infrastructure

2. Cooperation between partners can be cumbersome as each entity has their own diverging interests

3. Due to the limit of mutual trust the partnerships must remain small so as not to overwhelm

4. With the involvement of government agencies there is a lack of international involvement

5. Core functions of the government cannot be outsourced

It is with these five issues limitations are starting to be seen with the use of the public-private partnership model and may limit the usage of the model.

To adequately address the limitations of the model, it was necessary for the public-private partnerships roles and responsibilities to be determined (Givens and Busch, 2013). Coordination and trust was necessary as private partners were hesitant to cooperate, as partners did not wish to share deficiencies in hardware where competitors could use this information in day-to-day business dealings (2012). To combat this, a level of trust is needed between the partners especially those who compete in the same marketplace (Brechbuhl et al, 2010). For this level of trust to succeed the sector partners are looking for adequate incentives to allow for this level of collaboration (Federal Register, 2013; IT SCC, 2013; McConnell, 2013; Wildman, 2013; Canfield and Ward, 2013; IT SCC, 2013; Rupy and Mayer, 2013; Chessen, Polk, Podey, Symons, and Harvie, 2013; Coffey, Srihari, and Scarpelli, 2013).

The shared infrastructure utilized within the United States is more vulnerable to disruptions (NIPP, 2010). These disruptions can have several causes attributed to human error, not utilizing industry best practices, natural causes, terrorist/state-sponsored attacks or other malicious intent (2010). Numerous vendors are responsible for managing these networks further compounding the issues (2010). The partners working together and promoting the advantages of sharing information will allow for quicker responses to events and challenges limiting disruptions or compounding of issues (Brechbuhl et al, 2010). This sharing will also allow for the preserving of privacy for citizens, maintain constraints on government access to private information, and keep from private entities engaging in anti-competitive practices (Daniel, 2014).

These networks are necessary for the communications sector to allow first responders to obtain information as well as get information out to those needing it most in times of crisis (NIPP, 2010). Another challenge of using this type of partnership is it can be difficult to manage the partnership effectively (Clinton, 2011). Reasons why managing these partnerships can be difficult can range from a lack of coordination of responsibilities and/or failures of communication (2011). Clinton (2011) adds complexities organizations face purely on human interaction as assumptions' managing the partnership becomes more difficult and unruly.

Clinton (2011) also addressed the effect that even though the public-private partnership model can encounter difficulties it is impossible for one partner to take control and force the others to bend at will. The partners need to remain committed to the relationship and continue to progress by understanding, adapting and evolving towards the common goal (Clinton, 2011). These partnerships have to ensure public mandates or recommendations do not over reach the required expectations (Busch & Givens, 2012). Clear-cut expectations as to workforce strength, procurement of resources and management must stay clear of cost overruns otherwise those issues need to be addressed (2012).

Busch and Givens (2012) also agreed on the necessity of transparency both for the public sector to Congress as well as in the privatization of national security. Ridley (2011) likewise determined for this partnership to be less challenging it would be better for private partners of critical infrastructures to be able to use disclosed information purely for protection purposes and not for competitive advantage. With the launch of the cybersecurity framework, voluntary adoption is necessary and the main players must work together as cyber-protection is a team sport (Daniel, 2014). The partners need to provide feedback to make the process work (2014). Thus, the process is in need of a truly crosscutting approach by the participants only then will the process work (Daniel, 2012).

### Conclusion

This review, highlighted more detail of the application of the public-private partnership model's usefulness in the protection of critical infrastructure. The literature defined the public-private partnership which is an agreement between two entities one being a private sector business and the other a public or government agency allowing for a collaboration and combination of resources, skills and personnel to develop or in the case of critical infrastructures to protect a technology (Cellucci, 2010). Grossman (2012) also spoke to how public-private partnerships were becoming more mainstream policy for governments allowing private sector talent to grow while allowing the public sector to protect the populous. This chapter looked at the history of the public-private partnership model dating back to colonial times of United States history through to its current present day usage.

This review continued with the introduction of the National Infrastructure Protection Plan and the necessity of this protection plan to touch upon the fact no single

Federal agency or private organization owns the Internet but the protection of the Internet is a national and global challenge, which requires cooperation across both the private and public sector (Maughan, 2010). Hall (2012) spoke to the necessity of partner cooperation in critical infrastructure protections was the greatest strength of the Internet. This is because of the fact that multiple private partners involved in those infrastructures have resources to aid in its protection. Such co-operation is necessary because both the private and public sectors are completely dependent of one another but share equally the responsibility to protect critical infrastructure (Maughan, 2010). To meet the challenges presented to the protection of critical infrastructure the Federal government elected to reach out to the owners of critical infrastructures in an effort to build a risk management solution private industries could adapt to better assess risk, prioritize needs and to execute the necessary protective measures (Stephan, 2006). This was the basis of the National Infrastructure Protection Plan.

The literature review looked at the communications sector of the plan. The communications sector has evolved over time from wireline communications to systems now relying on a highly competitive industry of interconnected services encompassing wireless, satellite, cable, and broadcast companies offering similar services (NIPP, 2010). The review looked at what shaped the communications sector, and in particular at two key events. The first was the breakup of AT&T in 1984 and the second was the creation of the Telecommunications Act of 1996 (NIPP, 2010). These two events allowed for de-regulation of key communications companies and the competitive marketplace we currently see today.

While the private sector industries own the majority of the critical infrastructure it is the public sector who is responsible for supporting those systems critical to defense, law enforcement and public safety and it is this interdependence has increase the necessity of upgrades to these critical infrastructures (NIPP, 2010). This allowed for a collaborative effect of public partners working with private partner equals. The collaborative effort between public and private sectors established the best practices in infrastructure protection. The collaborative effort will be a deterrent to criminal or state-sponsored entities that might otherwise seek to stage attacks or engage in cybercrime (Garcia, 2006).

The literature review then concluded by looking at the challenges faced by partners in the communications sector and the protection of critical infrastructure. The challenges were areas such as lack of clear communications between its partners and the reluctance to share information because of competitive advantage. There are the fears of fines from the government partners for inadequacies and a general lack of coordination between partners in both sectors. Commitment issues between partners are another issue as well as transparency between not only the private sector partners but also the public sector partners. It was here the literature review for the purpose of this research topic concluded.

## Summary

In summary, the literature review looked at the both the past and current literature centered on the public-private partnership model. In particular, the areas focused on the need for critical infrastructure protection, history of the public-private partnership model and the currently used models. The review continued by also looking at the history of the

National Infrastructure Protection Plan, how the plan focuses on the communication sector, and finally looked at the public-private partnership usage within the communication sector and challenges it poses. The public-private partnership model was reviewed from its historical beginnings and continued through its use in the Department of Homeland Security's plans for critical infrastructure protections (NIPP Communications Sector Overview). The transition allowed the review to focus on the Homeland Security Presidential Directive 7 (HSPD-7). The HSPD-7 directive was designed around the protection of the sixteen most critical infrastructures within the United States.

Some of the key points coming out of this review are the criticality of critical infrastructure protection because the Internet has no political or geographic boundaries and countries are going to have to work together and share cyber security responsibilities (Brechbuhl et al, 2010). Nowhere was this more apparent than with the cyber-attacks on critical infrastructure in Estonia's or prior to the Russian invasion of Georgia, this just highlights how linked the entire world is (Glennon, 2012). The public-private partnership model use from before the formation of the United States continuing to this day addresses another key point and Garvin (2012) stated the public-private partnership model has been considered the most significant trend within the public sector. Meidute and Paliulis (2011) reiterated a principle driver in utilizing a public-private partnership was due to the efficiency of performing the necessary functions not typically possessed by the public sector. This is shown with the three approaches reviewed for this study: Garvin's P3 Equilibrium Model, Ahmad and Yuno's Cyber Terrorism Conceptual Framework and the most recent completed by the National Institute of Standards and Technology's Cybersecurity Framework.

The National Infrastructure Protection Plan was introduced as collaboration between the Department of Homeland Sector with other Federal agencies and the private sector. This was necessary as Maughan (2010) noted no single Federal agency or private organization owned the Internet but the protection of the Internet is a national and global challenge, which requires cooperation across both the private and public sector. The National Infrastructure Protection Plan looks to utilize the new cybersecurity framework, which was created out of a White House Executive Order and backed by the efforts to create a seamless national backbone for digital capacity (DHS Executive Order 13636, 2013). The framework utilizes the public-private partnership to share responsibilities across sector partners, sharing information critical for protection and incident response and creating future innovation (Grossman, 2012). This basis sets the cornerstones of critical infrastructure protection.

In the next chapter, this study will look to the research methods to be utilized in determining how security frameworks designed using the public-private partnership model aid in the protection of critical infrastructure. By utilizing a survey the researcher will be able to discuss with those individuals within the critical infrastructures sectors their opinions and feelings on the current model.

## CHAPTER 3: RESEARCH METHODS

The purpose of this study was to determine how security frameworks designed using the public-private partnership model aid in identifying suggested security best practices for Company XYZ's critical infrastructure within the United States. The research method selected for this dissertation was an exploratory case study. This research design allowed for a qualitative analysis using interviews with pre-defined questions about the public-private partnership model. While significant research has been conducted regarding critical infrastructure in general, there is a lack or absence of academic research on determining how security frameworks designed using the public-private partnership model aid in identifying suggested security best practices. As a result, an exploratory case model was appropriate for this study.

The remainder of this chapter will provide a full elaboration of the method of research being utilized for this project. It begins with a look at the design and appropriateness to this study. Then the research question to be answered with this research, the population, sample criteria, data collection, and the instrument to obtain it was examined. The validity and reliability of the results was discussed and finally the techniques to analyze the data were discussed. The chapter summary will complete this chapter with a brief overview and an introduction to Chapter 4.

### Research Method and Design Appropriateness

When looking at this dissertation, "The Public-Private Partnership Model: Identifying Security Best Practices for Critical Infrastructure" it should be noted that very little research has been performed on determining how security frameworks designed using the public-private partnership model aid in identifying suggested security best practices for Company XYZ's critical infrastructure within the United States. The criticality of looking into the topic is highlighted by the fact the United States Department of Homeland Security has put this partnership model front and center with the design of the National Infrastructure Protection Plan (NIPP, 2013). The Department of Homeland Security has added to this study's necessity by supporting the design of the new NIST Cybersecurity Framework, which is being slated as the standard security best practice for the protection of critical infrastructure (NIST, 2013). For this study to build a theory on a concept that has not been determined means this dissertation looked at all of the research surrounding this phenomenon and sought input from partners within the private sector to get their feedback. Input was needed to determine if the lack of standardized security best practices to protect critical infrastructure from cyberattacks is adequately addressed by utilizing the public-private partnership model and one of its associated frameworks. Then determine how security frameworks designed using this model aid in the identification of suggested security best practices to protect Company XYZ's critical infrastructure. For these reasons the decision was made to use an exploratory case study to allow Company XYZ to determine how security frameworks designed using the public-private partnership model aid in the organization's current security best practice identification.

Given the purpose of this study was to determine how the security frameworks designed using the public-private partnership model aid in identifying suggested security best practices for Company XYZ's critical infrastructure within the United States, the most suitable research method was an exploratory case study using interviews from a critical infrastructure organization. Performing a qualitative analysis with the use of a case study, as the method is appropriate for this study, as the case study approach allowed for the candid capturing of input from the study's participants (Yin, 2014). The case study also added two additional sources of evidence the first being direct observation of the participant and the second being the data collected during the interviews of the participant (Yin, 2014). This research design method allowed for a qualitative analysis of interview responses from a critical infrastructure organization. Another reason why an exploratory case study fit well within this study and was appropriate is easily seen in the fact there is research around critical infrastructure but a complete lack of academic research around determining how security frameworks designed using the public-private partnership model aid in identifying suggested security best practices. Finally, the use of an exploratory case study allowed the researcher to explore a critical problem the data currently does not define (Stebbins, 2001).

## Research Question

**Research Question**

The dissertation presented a research question which will be answered in Chapter 4. The research question concerns the best way to protect critical infrastructure in the United States by identifying suggested security best practices. The public and private sectors need to ensure there is full protection of these critical resources from both outside and inside attacks. The research question this study will address is, " Is the lack of identifying suggested security best practices to protect critical infrastructure from cyberattacks adequately addressed by utilizing the public-private partnership model and frameworks designed using that model?"

**Interview Questions**

Yin (2012) stated that exploratory case studies allow the participants to have active involvement in identifying issues with a problem not clearly defined. To that end, the researcher provided the participants questions that supplied the researcher the necessary information to answer the study's questions. These questions were asked using oral interviews and are provided in Appendix F. Below the researcher has provided an in-depth look at each of the participant's questions used in this case study.

1. Who in Company XYZ is responsible for developing and implementing organization-wide cybersecurity protective measures (devices, policy, etc.) and is this the right or wrong person, explain? The first question will provide information to the researcher as to who determines what security measures are put in place and defines what are security best practices.

2. How is Company XYZ's senior leadership informed about cyber risk and its impact on the overall business and is the input gained from their expertise/experience utilized to identify security best practices? The second question tries to further ascertain who leads security best practice identification.

3. What benefits could Company XYZ gain by utilizing role-specific training around security awareness, incident response, and threat assessment? Will this aid in identifying security best practices? The third question looks to see what the consensus is around role-specific training and if it aids in identifying the necessary security best practices for Company XYZ.

4. As part of Company XYZ's proactive security posture, what benefits could the organization gain by determining, reviewing, and protecting critical data/systems?

The fourth question will see what the participant feels are benefits to protecting critical data/infrastructure within Company XYZ.

5. How does self-assessment of cyber protection capabilities aid Company XYZ and/or would a third party or best practice sharing system be more suited to aid in the identification of security best practices? The fifth question starts to ask whether the participant thinks that a public-private partnership information sharing service could aid in identifying security best practices.

6. To aid in identifying security best practices should Company XYZ actively participate in information sharing forums with other critical infrastructure partners and what benefits can be gained by doing so? The sixth question seeks to determine if Company XYZ could gain benefits to sharing information with other critical infrastructure partners.

7. Would the sharing of both attempted and successful intrusions attempts on Company XYZ with other critical infrastructure partners, through an information-sharing forum, lend itself to identifying security best practices to protect from Company XYZ from similar attacks in the future and is this sharing a good idea? The seventh question raises the question of how much sharing should be allowed and if there are any benefits or inherent risks with giving out the information.

8. Do you think that information sharing with other critical infrastructure partners could allow Company XYZ to be more vulnerable to cyberattack? Why or why not? The eighth question looks to obtain further participant feedback on the whether or not sharing information through a public-private partnership information sharing forum will aid in identify security best practices.

9. Do you think that proper preparation for future incidents, including information sharing, will aid Company XYZ's effort to properly identify security best practices to protect it? Why or why not? The ninth question is gaining insight into the future of security best practice identification.

10. What other methods can Company XYZ utilize to aid in identifying security best practices to protect its critical infrastructure? The tenth question looks for the participant to provide any additional information the researcher could use for this study and to aid in the determination of future research.

### Instrumentation

For this study, a case study was implemented, which generated artifacts ranging from electronic documents, interviews, and direct observation (Yin, 2014). These artifacts were collected throughout the study and entered into the case study database for analysis. The technique of interviews used in this single-phase case study provided the necessary information to address the research questions posed within this dissertation. The case study protocol outlined in Appendix D was an effective means for assessing the issue at hand surrounding the determination of how security frameworks designed using the public-private partnership model aid in identifying suggested security best practices (2014). Single-phase case studies follow one of five rationales thus it is critical, unusual, common, revelatory or longitudinal (2014). The rationale surrounds the effectiveness of the single-phase case study being conducted here centers around a common rationale. The common rationale's objective was to capture data around an everyday situation (security best-practice design) to allow lessons to be learned (2014). The case study protocol guided the researcher with outlining the rules and procedures to be followed.

Yin (2014) outlined a case study with three major parts identified as the collection of evidence, following a proper chain of custody, and the usage of a database to store the evidence. Yin (2014) also stated that when collecting evidence for a case study there are typically six sources. The six sources collected are comprised of physical artifacts, documentation, direct and participant observations, interviews, and finally archival records (2014). For the purposes of this study, the instrument looked at data collected during the interviews, direct observation (Illinois), and indirect observation (Georgia and Colorado). The data collected was then coded for further analysis in Chapter 4.

This case study utilized coding of the data to be collected. The researcher coded the data in a single cycle. Saldana (2009) discussed the process of evaluation coding as a way to apply non-quantitative codes onto qualitative data. This allows judgments about the merit and worth of programs and policies to be assigned (2009). Evaluation data can describe, compare, and predict and for the purposes of this study, a description is needed to focus on observation and responses from the interview participants (2009).

Evaluation coding is appropriate for policy, critical, action, organizational and evaluation studies (Saldana, 2009). This study was determining how security frameworks designed using the public-private partnership model aid in the design of suggested security best practices. This case study used three elements in the coding of data: magnitude codes, In Vivo (or descriptive) codes, and recommendation (REC) code (2009). The magnitude codes determined the positive or negative responses of the participant, the In Vivo code gave a brief description of the response, and REC code flagged the response with a memo/action for follow-up (2009). The coding aided in answering the research question by determining how the public-private partnership model is perceived in designing suggested security best practices. For this case study, the researcher used the Data Summary Matrix shown in Table 1. The use of this table allowed for a breakdown of the answers from the studies participants and allowed the researcher to determine future research.

Table 1

*Data Summary Matrix*

| Date | Question # | Magnitude (+/-) | In Vivo (Description) | REC (Recommendation) |
|------|-----------|-----------------|----------------------|----------------------|
| | | | | |

The instrument for this case study was comprised of the case study protocol, chain of custody, and the database. The database was used as the central repository for the artifacts collected throughout this study. The usage of this instrument was determined to be a reliable instrument (Yin, 2014). The instrument provided the researcher with qualitative results, while using the case study protocol, to allow for viable insight into suggested security best practice design.

**Validity and Reliability**

When looking at the study one of the most important things a researcher must look at is the validity of the study. According to Creswell (2012), validity is the development of evidence that demonstrates the interpretation of test results matches the proposed test. Salkind (2012) further defines validity in terms of whether the test or instrument the researcher is using in the study actually measures what was intended. Stebbins (2001) defines validity as the credibility that researchers gain by achieving an accurate or true impression of the study and how it can be accomplished. The threats to this validity are due to the fact the researcher may make the incorrect inferences during the study (Creswell, 2012). The issues of validity cross four thresholds of construct validity, internal validity, external validity, and reliability.

**Construct Validity**

Construct validity is defined as the validity of inferences about the constructs of the study (Creswell, 2012; Salkind, 2012). Construct validity is also the determination of the significance; the means; the purpose; and the use of scores form a study's instrument (2012). According to Yin (2014), construct validity should use multiple sources of evidence, establish a chain of custody, and finally have the participants review the final version of the case study report. During this study, the researcher chose to validate the construct validity during the data collection phase.

**Internal Validity**

This study was an exploratory design and lacked an independent variable; however, internal validity was still considered. Internal validity is defined as the degree to which the study's results can be attributed to the independent variable. Internal validity is used heavily in experimental designs where the research looks to see if what the researcher sees is a function of what they did; if it is then they have valid internal validity (Salkind, 2012). Meltzoff (2010) goes further as the researcher needs to determine if the results found were truly attributed to the experiment. The threats to internal validity are the issues in drawing the correct inferences between the variables and the intended outcome (Creswell, 2012). There are primarily three categories of threats to internal validity. The first addresses participants, the second is the treatments, and finally there are the procedures used for the study (Creswell, 2012).

For this exploratory research study, the first category of threat to internal validity was necessary as it relates to the procedures used during the study. This first category addressed the testing and instrumentation (Creswell, 2012). The second category of threat to internal validity was testing. With testing the researcher needed to ensure that the study's respondents did not become familiar with the outcome measures and its responses (Creswell, 2012). Creswell (2012) continues the discussion on internal validity by looking at the third category of threat to internal validity, instrumentation. Instrumentation was a threat to internal validity because the instrument could have changed from the pilot testing to the final testing.

To ensure internal validity of the study the researcher needed to ensure that the participants did not share information regarding the study. The researcher also had to keep from making any inferences to any event that was not directly observed (Yin, 2014). A researcher typically makes inferences that an event resulted from an earlier occurrence (2014). To ensure that internal validity is maintained the researcher needed to address and anticipate questions around the inference to ensure that it is correct by using pattern matching, explanation building, rival explanations and by using logic models (2014).

**External Validity**

In this exploratory study the other validity, issue a researcher looked at is external validity. External validity constitutes ways a researcher could generalize the results of the study and to what extent. Salkind (2012) also states external validity results will allow for a generalization from sample to sample and then to the whole population. Meltzoff (2010) further defines external validity by reaffirming that the study's results would be the same outside of the particular situation. The threats to external validity were those problems threatening the researcher's ability to draw the correct inferences for the data samples to other variables such as people, settings, and measures (Creswell, 2012). There are three threats typically affecting a studies generalizability and they are: selection and treatment, setting and treatment and history and treatment (Creswell, 2012). Selection and treatment refers to the inability to generalize beyond the groups used in the experiment (Creswell, 2012). Creswell (2012) continues with the threat of setting and treatment involves the inability of the study to be generalized to different settings. Finally, Creswell (2012) discusses the threat of history and treatment that develops when a researcher tries to generalize the findings to past or future events.

For this exploratory research study, selection, and treatment are the main points that needed to be looked at. The reasoning behind this is the study needed to ensure the results could be generalized across the different critical infrastructure sectors and not just to the communications sector. As the researcher was not concerned solely with the usage of the public-private partnership model for critical infrastructure protection, the concern of setting was not a foreseen threat to external validity. In addition, since this exploratory study is new research there was no concern of generalizability from past situations.

**Reliability**

Salkind (2012) and Stebbins (2001) define reliability in terms of the likelihood a test measures the same thing more than once will produce the same result when repeated and whether or not another researcher with similar training and understanding of the subject matter can make the same observations. Creswell (2012) also states that reliability of an instrument stable and consistent. The reliability of the case study was validated by the data collection phase of the study (Yin, 2014). Yin (2014) states the objective of reliability is to ensure any future researcher who follows the same set of procedures used in this study will arrive at the same findings and conclusions the earlier researcher did. The way the researcher gets to this was by generalizing the steps of the process in a way that is easily repeatable like someone was looking over the researcher's shoulder and recording the process (2014). Each of the tests for this case study was built upon Yin's criteria for judging the quality of a research design (2014). The tests follow the process of construct validity, internal validity, external validity, and reliability. The use of the four tests provided the necessary constructs for a viable case study and are common to all social science research methods (2014).

## Population and Sampling

### Population

The general population for this study was a geographically diverse group of individuals from within a Department of Homeland Security designated critical infrastructure sector. The fifteen employees were from within the Information Technology department from locations in Naperville, Illinois, Denver, Colorado, and West Point, Georgia. To add additional guidelines to the study's population it was stated that the group interviewed for this case was from the Information Technology department (Salkind, 2012). To complete a study effectively a sample needs to be selected from this population but it must be done in a way to maximize the likelihood the sample reflects the characteristics of the total population (2012). For the purposes of this study, the sample was collected from a group of fifteen employees working within Company XYZ. Each of these individuals are involved on a daily basis with the protection of the critical infrastructure as well as intimately familiar with security best practice design in Company

XYZ. According to Salkind (2012), the surroundings of the population and sample are just as important to the research as the individual interaction. The selection of these fifteen employees allowed for a sound case study, as these individuals are responsible for driving best practices within Company XYZ.

This study sought to observe the individuals interviewed for this case study within the natural work environment. This allowed for a more concise determination on the environmental factors on identifying suggested security best practices and how the individuals choose to engage the public-private partnership as well as to the partnership's usage in the organization. The observations made by the researcher here determined how the management perceives the partnership model, how the organization chooses to design suggested security best practices and direction for future research into this topic. The geographic locations for this study will be centered on Company XYZ's three primary information technology hubs. The first is in Naperville, Illinois; the second in Denver, Colorado, and the third is located in West Point, Georgia. The researcher conducted the case study from a virtual environment for the participants in West Point, Georgia and Denver Colorado but was working directly with participants from within the Naperville, Illinois location.

## Confidentiality

Salkind (2012) best summarized the ethics in research by stating confidentiality is only maintained when learned participant data is held in the strictest of confidence. The data needs to be kept disguised, as this will allow anonymity to be maintained throughout the collection and publication process (Salkind, 2012). Appendix E provides the confidentiality statement that was presented to all study participants of this case study.

This confidentiality statement ensured that the participants understand their rights and will serve as their informed consent. The interview participants were given the option to be interviewed or not and as part of their informed consent were given the option to withdraw from the study at any time. This case study was not collecting any personally identifiable information, as it has no bearing on the outcome of the research study. The researcher ensured no personally identifiable information was collected or stored within the case study's database. When interviews were conducted, the researcher coded the individuals as follows in Table 2:

Table 2

*Strategy for Coding Participants*

| Column A - Human Subject | Column B - Coded Participant |
|---|---|
| Junior/Senior Team Member | P1 thru P15 |

Note: The researcher interviewed human subjects. This table provides the method used by the researcher to code those human subjects. Column A contains the seniority of the subject and Column B depicts the coding used to protect the participant's identity.

Table 2 depicts how the researcher facilitated the coding of the participants of this case study and thus protected the identity of the participant. In Column A, labeled as "Human Subject" the researcher provided only the seniority of the participant using the names of Junior or Senior Team Member, this added an element of confidentiality for the participant. In Column B, labeled as "Coded Participant" the researcher provided a participant number only and this was followed sequentially through the study for each of the participants. The case study included interviews from fifteen employees within the information technology department of Company XYZ. Participants were provided instructions to discuss only the ten provided questions, which pertained to this case study.

Any communications with the participants was de-identified when stored in the case study database.

## Data Collection

The data collection methods for this study included artifacts collected during one-on-one interviews, participant observations, and documents (Yin, 2014). The collection of artifacts allowed the researcher to obtain information to adequately answer the study's main research questions. These artifacts built the baseline for this qualitative exploratory case study. The coding was applied to the various artifacts and stored in the case study database.

The interviews were one of the most important pieces of evidence collected (Yin, 2014). To adequately complete the interview process the researcher needed to follow their own line of inquiry and ask questions in an unbiased manner (2014). The other element was to engage in participant observation, which was challenging to the researcher as it can introduce bias into the study but can also yield some unique insight (2014). Finally, documentation was obtained in many forms during the study and is best if they can corroborate and augment evidence from other sources (2014). It is through the usage of these artifact types the researcher was able to put together a convergence of evidence such as in Figure 5 (2014). It is through the convergence of evidence the data was used to strengthen the construct validity of the case study as multiple evidence types were being utilized (2014).

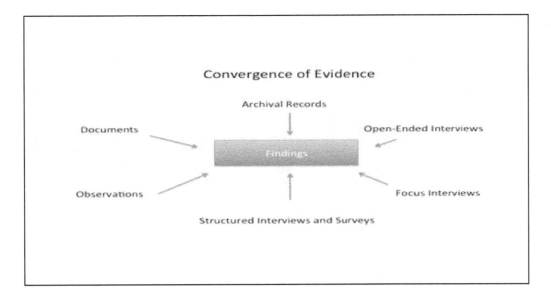

*Figure 5.* Convergence of Evidence (Yin, 2014). Adapted from "Case study research: Design and Methods" *by* R. K. Yin, R. K., 2014.

With the convergence of evidence, the data collection process will be almost complete with the addition of the case study database, a properly maintained chain of evidence, and an exercise of caution when using electronic sources (Yin, 2014).

The rationale behind the design of the study to use interviews, observations, and documents was built around the decision of the researcher to not look at archival records, conduct surveys, or utilize focused interviews. Usage of archival records was not possible as little to no research was available in identifying suggested security best practices around critical infrastructure. A survey was a possible option but lacked a direct observation element that the researcher needed to aid in the design of running themes. Finally, focused interviews would have allowed for an element of bias by the researcher as the questions would not adequately allow the participant to answer the question in their own terms.

## Data Analysis

Data analysis, according to Creswell (2012), is the process of describing the trends, comparison of groups, or the relative values by using statistical analysis. Data analysis typically consists of collecting, organizing, and preparing the data collected during the research process. This data will then be presented into an understandable medium to the intended audience (Creswell, 2012). For the purposes of this study, the data was collected by using interviews comprised of several questions probing the participants for information relevant to determining how security frameworks designed using the public-private partnership model aid in designing suggested security best practices for Company XYZ's critical infrastructure within the United States. The interviews were designed to solicit responses from personnel at Company XYZ regarding their perceptions and knowledge of the public-private partnership model, how security frameworks designed using the model protect critical infrastructure, and identifying suggested security best practices.

This case study used a single-phase approach to coding data in this qualitative exploratory case study. This approach allowed the researcher to take the collected interview data and categorize it into the case study database. The type of coding for this case study followed what is called evaluation coding which fits well in this study as this study reflected an evaluation study (Saldana, 2009). The data will use three elements for coding: magnitude codes, In Vivo (or descriptive) codes, and recommendation (REC) code (Saldana, 2009). The magnitude code determined the positive or negative responses of the participant, the In Vivo code gave a brief description of the response, and REC code flagged the response with a memo/action for follow-up (2009). The coding allowed the researcher to correlate the responses of the participants to gain valuable insight into the public-private partnerships and usage for creating suggested security best practices. This type of coding allowed the researcher to analyze the data collected from the participant to answer the study's central research question. The analytical technique that will be used in this study was a parallel procedure to what is called explanation building, which for this exploratory case study allowed the researcher to develop ideas that could be used for future research (Yin, 2014). Yin's (2014) explanation building allows for the explanation of a phenomenon, as the researcher will utilize insight of the study's participants to gain an understanding of creating suggested best practices.

In conclusion, interviews were conducted to investigate and obtain information from Company XYZ with intimate knowledge of the use of the public-private partnership model within the guidelines of the National Infrastructure Protection Plan. The responses aided in the determination of how security frameworks designed using the public-private partnership model aid in designing suggested security best practices for Company XYZ's critical infrastructure within the United States. These responses allowed the researcher to determine how the public-private partnership model is perceived by a critical infrastructure. Saldana (2009) spoke to issues of researcher objectivity with this type of study but that the research can be effective if the participants of the study are relied on, particularly what they say and do. These perceptions of the model aided the researcher in determine future research of this topic.

**Summary**

The purpose of the qualitative exploratory case study was to determine how security frameworks designed using the public-private partnership model aid in identifying suggested security best practices for Company XYZ's critical infrastructure within the United States. Chapter 3 provided an explanation of the research methodology and its design appropriateness to this study (Yin, 2014). The chapter continued by addressing the research question for the study, the instrumentation and its reliability, the population of individuals for the study, geographic location, and sampling method (Creswell, 2012; Yin, 2014; Saldana, 2009; and Salkind, 2012). Finally, the chapter concluded with the discussion around the data analysis to be used in the study.

In the next chapter, the study will go over the pilot study and its results. It will then look at the observations and data gained during the remaining interviews as well as any direct, management, operational, and informal observations. It will be through these observations that themes will be determined to aid in best practice identification.

## CHAPTER 4: RESULTS

The purpose of this study was to determine how security frameworks designed utilizing the public-private partnership model aid in the identification of suggested security best practices for a telecommunications provider's (Company XYZ) critical infrastructure within the United States. The examination was conducted through a series of interviews and observations of Company XYZ employees. The research presented in Chapters 1 and 2 showed the current lack of academic research on the security frameworks designed using the public-private partnership model. This case study research included interviews, a literature review, and direct observations of the local participants, as some of the participants interviewed were located in remote locations.

### Pilot Study

The purpose behind the pilot study was for the researcher to establish the reliability and validity of the interview questions selected for this study. While conducting the pilot study, the researcher ensured the correct elements to answer the study's research question were addressed. The pilot study consisted of four preliminary interviews regarding suggested best practice identification within Company XYZ while one participant asked to be removed from the study. The results from the pilot study led the researcher to make changes to the method of facilitation of the interviews, and to the method of presenting participants with the interview questions, in addition, the researcher decided to switch from handwritten notes to capturing the interview notes using Microsoft Word to improve the overall collection process. Appendix G - Pilot Study Results, presents the raw findings of the pilot study.

The researcher conducted three interviews using the interview questions located in Appendix F - Interview Questions for Case Study. The participants' answers were rated as either being a satisfactory or unsatisfactory response. Observations of the participants during the facilitation of the interview were noted and adjusted to remove any unwanted outcomes as previously identified through the pilot study.

## Findings

The study identified avenues for suggested security best practice creation within a telecommunications company applying security frameworks designed using the public-private partnership model. The case study took a single-phased approach to code the data collected in this qualitative exploratory case study. The researcher took the coded data and categorized it in within a database. The data included all of the interview question responses, length of service within Company XYZ of the participant and whether or not the questions were adequately addressed. After placing all of the data into the database, the researcher sorted the responses into themes. These themes proved to be beneficial to identifying suggested security best practices for Company XYZ.

**Interviews**

Ten open-ended interview questions were presented to each case study participant and are provided in Chapter 3 and Appendix F – Interview Questions for Case Study for reference. After initial analysis of each participant's interview responses, the researcher analyzed the data. After the data was coded, a thematic analysis was performed to seek broader themes that would help to identify suggested security best practices for Company XYZ; a telecommunication provider deemed a critical infrastructure within the United States by the Department of Homeland Security.

The researcher conducted fifteen interviews in the case study. Originally, there were supposed to be twenty-eight interviews, but thirteen of the participants declined to participate in the study. Thirteen participants were unable to participate due to time constraints. Information given to each participant is provided in Appendix E – Case Study Consent Form (Informed Consent) and Appendix F – Interview Questions for Case Study. The researcher transcribed all of the interviews, then the data was entered into a database, and patterns were generated from the participant responses and placed into themes.

## Method of Selection

The goal of the study was 100% participation of the case study participants. Company XYZ provided the email addresses, phone numbers, and names of the participants for the case study. The researcher informed all of the participants about the case study and requested participation via email. There was no effort to exclude any Company XYZ employee from the opportunity to participate. Separate follow up emails were sent to the participants seeking their support to be interviewed. The participants were interested to participate in the study; however, the eight who did not participate failed to respond to the researcher's requests.

### General Interviewee Information

Table 3 offers general information regarding the participants. Originally, the population consisted of twenty-eight participants. Thirteen of those participants declined to participate in the study. Only fifteen individuals elected to participate in the case study. Of the fifteen, eleven were senior employees of Company XYZ (73%) and four were junior employees of Company XYZ (27%).

Table 3

*Subject Coding in Database*

| **Human Subjects** | **Coded Participant** |
| --- | --- |
| Senior | Pilot1 |
| Senior | Pilot2 |
| Senior | Pilot3 |
| Junior | P1 |
| Junior | P2 |
| Senior | P3 |
| Senior | P4 |
| Junior | P5 |
| Senior | P6 |
| Senior | P7 |
| Senior | P8 |
| Junior | P9 |
| Senior | P10 |
| Senior | P11 |
| Senior | P12 |

The interview questions were designed to gain a general understanding of the participant's experience with suggested security best practices and general insight into how those suggested best practices might be identified in Company XYZ.

**Emerging Themes from Data Collection**

The data collected by the researcher from the interviews yielded ways in which Company XYZ could identify suggested security best practices. Coding analysis was conducted to ensure accuracy of the data and the themes generated from the data collected. The results of the coding are provided below as a list of recurring themes that presented themselves from the participant's responses. The themes are as follows:

1. Responsible Parties for Suggested Best Practice Identification

2. Senior Management Involvement and Knowledge

3. Security Training

4. Proactive Security

5. Security Assessments

6. Information Sharing with Partners

7. Future Preparation

8. Alternative Methods

These themes had common responses by almost all of the participants, which suggested to the researcher that the participants were keenly aware of what was necessary to identify suggested security best practices within Company XYZ. Additionally, the responses also demonstrated that current utilization of the public-private partnership model for the identification of suggested security best practices was not in use within Company XYZ.

**Research Question**

The research question sought to identify suggested security best practices using the security frameworks designed using the public-private partnership model to protect Company XYZ's critical infrastructure. The evidence collected from the interviews and literature review produced the following eight themes in Table 4.

Table 4

*Themes for Identifying Suggested Security Best Practices*

| Theme | Title | General Comments |
|---|---|---|
| Theme 1 | Responsible Parties for Best Practice Identification | "The Security Team should be the primary party responsible for overall best practice identification." 93% of the participants agreed with this theme. |
| Theme 2 | Senior Management Involvement and Knowledge | "The Security Team informs the Senior Leadership as well as what they obtain from security media outlets." 87% of the participants agreed with this theme. |
| Theme 3 | Security Training | "Role based training yields suggested security best practice designs within the organization." 100% of the participants agreed with this theme. |
| Theme 4 | Proactive Security | "Proactively addressing security needs benefits the organization and it leads to suggested security best practice creation." 100% of the participants agreed with this theme. |
| Theme 5 | Security Assessments | "Internal and external assessments used together would allow the business to identify suggested security best practices." 87% of the participants agreed with this theme. |
| Theme 6 | Information Sharing with Partners | "Sharing with sector partners is a good idea and leads to identifying suggested security best practices but some reservations need to be made in regards to the depth of information shared." 67% of the participants agreed with this theme. |
| Theme 7 | Future Preparation | "Preparation for the future always leads to the identification of suggested security best practices." 93% of the participants agreed with this theme. |
| Theme 8 | Alternative Methods | "Communication between the business and its employees as well as with other partners will continue to identify suggested security best practices." 67% of the participants agreed with this theme. |

Table 4 outlines the overall analysis of the coded data collected during the

interviews. The first column is the theme column where the researcher identified eight themes while coding the interview data. The second column, title, provided the name that the researcher gave to the running theme from the responses. The third column, general comments, provided a generalized comment based on the stated percentages of the participant's responses during the interview. In the following sections, each theme is broken down in greater depth to provide more detailed information gained during the interviews, and the relevance to the research question.

**Theme 1:**

*Representative comment.* "The Security Team should be the primary party responsible for overall suggested best practice identification" (Participant). The study revealed the security team was the primary driver of identifying suggested security best practices. Ninety-three percent of the participants of this case study stated this fact and the remainder felt that some ownership of the identification of suggested security best practices fell onto the shoulders of the business. The primary reason was the security team did not have the proper insight into all elements of the business.

**Theme 2:**

*Representative comment.* "The Security Team informs the Senior Leadership as well as what they obtain from media outlets" (Participant). The study revealed the senior leadership team's primary sources of identifying suggested security best practices comes from their faith in the security team and what they read or hear from media sources that they follow. Eighty-seven percent of the participants agreed with this statement with the remainder of the participants felt that the senior leadership team lacked information on suggested security best practice identification. The study revealed some participants felt the senior leadership team had no reference about security, cared more about the business making money, and did not know what was necessary to identify suggested security best practices to protect the business.

**Theme 3:**

*Representative comment.* "Role based training yields suggested security best practice designs within the organization" (Participant). The study revealed the participants felt that role-based security training was considerably more effective than umbrella security training to help identify suggested security best practices. One hundred percent of the participants agreed role based training would educate employees and allow them to be more effective in identifying both new and enhancements to suggested security best practices. The participants also noted that role-based training would also allow for quicker response times to incidents, and allow for better collaboration between teams. Then, the business could embrace suggested security best practices more effectively.

**Theme 4:**

*Representative comment.* "Proactively address security needs benefit the organization and leads to suggested best practice creation" (Participant). In theme four, the study revealed that any organization engaging in a proactive security posture would be better suited to identify additional suggested security best practices to protect itself. One hundred percent of the interviewed participants felt the business, if engaged with a proactive security posture, would be able to identify the necessary suggested security best practices to protect it. The responses also noted that, while the business was not currently establishing a proactive security posture, one could easily be adopted while allowing the business to better protect itself and its customers.

**Theme 5:**

*Representative comment.* "Internal and external assessments used together would allow the business to identify suggested security best practices" (Participant). The study revealed, in theme five, that a combination of both internal and external security assessments allowed the business to identify more as well as specific suggested security best practices to protect the business. Eighty-seven percent of the participants of the study felt that the combination approach allowed for the best collaborative approach of identified suggested security best practices. The remainder of the participants felt a third party external assessment would allow for better suggested best practice creation because they work with a multitude of clients, thus yielding more suggested security best practices.

**Theme 6:**

*Representative comment.* "Sharing with sector partners is a good idea and leads to identifying suggested security best practices but some reservations need to be made in regards to the depth of information shared" (Participant). The study revealed in theme six that sharing of identified suggested security best practices between sector partners as well as other critical infrastructure sectors would aid a business in best protecting itself. Sixty-seven percent of the study participants felt that partner sharing was good for Company XYZ as well as other business and allowed for the identification of suggested security best practices. The remainder of the participants had other feelings concerning the process.

The participants who did not fully agree with information sharing did not all have the same concerns. The concerns they voiced the data shared should be generalized to not allow for additional attacks or to show potential threat vectors. Another concern was around the nature of a shared attack and whether or not it was deemed as critical such as a denial of service attack or minimal such as a phishing campaign. The remainder questioned how a partner was vetted by the Department of Homeland Security to be allowed into the sharing program. If they are properly checked out and are indeed deemed a critical sector partner than, more sharing would be okay.

**Theme 7:**

*Representative comment.* "Preparation for the future always leads to the identification of suggested security best practices" (Participant). During the study theme seven showed that preparation for future attacks and incidents would allow for better identification of suggested security best practices. Ninety-three percent of the study's participants felt that early preparation would allow Company XYZ to be most prepared to guard against future incidents and attacks on the businesses critical infrastructure. The remainder of the participants felt that reliance on one internal group or external partners did not go far enough; they felt that better communication between all employees within the business and partners across multiple sectors would yield better methods of identifying suggested security best practices.

**Theme 8:**

*Representative comment.* "Communication between the business and its employees as well as with other partners will continue to identify suggested security best practices" (Participant). When the participants were asked about what could be done outside of the questions, the researcher had asked them, there was a consensus that communication was key to identifying suggested security best practices. Sixty-seven percent of the participants answered that better communications was the key to identifying suggested security best practices. The other participant responses stated that the identification of suggested security best practices was possible when there was a better understanding of the applications being utilized within the organization, proper policies were utilized throughout the organization, and that social media outlets were properly utilized to see what other organizations were suggesting as best practices to protect their critical systems.

Participants suggested a range of additional methods of identifying security best practices; these could yield a wealth of future research. One of these methods was the use of honeypots to lure attacks and learn from those attack vectors to identify suggested security best practices. There was a discussion of insider threats and how a business could utilize information gained from those attacks to identify suggested security best practices. The other element obtained in this question was how security should be allowed to create a cultural shift within the business. A cultural shift would allow the business to embrace suggested security best practices and would lead to the identification of additional suggested security best practices to protect critical infrastructure from cyberattacks.

## Summary

Chapter 4 presented the findings from this study. The research used interviews to gain an understanding of how Company XYZ identified suggested security best practices. The coded data was analyzed and categorized into eight themes. The themes aid in identifying suggested security best practices to protect critical infrastructure. In Chapter 5, the theoretical and practical implications of the findings obtained from these interviews will be discussed. The discussion in Chapter 5 will provide the necessary recommendations and implications from this data for its usage in future research. Chapter 5 outlined the recommendations and conclusions that the themes determined.

## CHAPTER 5: CONCLUSIONS AND RECOMMENDATIONS

The results of this study are significant to the information assurance field in that they can potentially aid organizations within the critical infrastructure space in identifying suggested security best practices to protect those services from attack. The significance of this exploratory case study is to determine how one organization within the communications sector of the Department of Homeland Security's critical infrastructure identified suggested security best practices within their organization, Company XYZ. The qualitative exploratory case study attempted to identify was that other organizations could identify suggested security best practices to protect critical infrastructure. This study was unique in that there is currently little to no academic research surrounding how security frameworks designed using the public-private partnership models aid in the identification of suggested security best practices as it relates to critical infrastructure protection of telecommunications providers.

Businesses such as Company XYZ are in competition on a daily basis and it seemed very unlikely that such an organization would be willing to freely share its security best practices. This is primarily because most businesses consider their security best practices confidential and proprietary information and sharing these security practices could allow a competitor to have an unfair advantage against the other in the marketplace. The themes generated from the participant interviews showed that the consensus could not be more wrong. Company XYZ is interested in sharing best practices as well as gaining additional insights into how to better identify suggested security best practices from their marketplace competitors. Where the issues lie is on how much information should be shared to ensure their competitive edge as well as protect

Company XYZ from liability. The study addresses this in the eight themes found while conducting interviews that will be discussed in more detail in the following sections.

A further significance of this study was the knowledge gained to help raise the visibility of critical infrastructure protection. The protection of critical infrastructures within the United States has become increasingly more visible with the introduction of large amounts of malware, bot networks, and infiltration from terrorist networks and rogue states, to name just a few examples. Earlier in this study, the discussion of rogue actors served to highlight the necessity of securing critical infrastructure. As discussed in Chapter 1, it was in early September 2014 that a resourceful terrorist organization, the Islamic State of Iraq and Syria (ISIS), was found to be working in collaboration with drug cartels (Gaffney, 2014). This collaboration was attempting to probe the critical electric grid where in June 2013 an improvised explosive was used to destroy an electric substation to determine how those substations handled the added stress of handling the larger capacity load placed on the other substations (Gaffney, 2014).

This study evaluated how security frameworks designed using the public-private partnership model aid in the identification of suggested security best practices and questioned whether the use of the public-private partnership model should continue in its current form or if the creation of a new model is necessary. The outcome from the participant interviews shows that this model, while not perfect, works to allow critical infrastructure partners to collaborate on identifying suggested security best practices. The private sector can benefit from these results, as it will allow the private sector to help in the determination of a model allowing for competiveness in the individual sectors. The private sector can also benefit from the results by being able to identify suggested security best practices for critical infrastructure protection using this model. The public sector will also benefit from this study as critical infrastructure partners become aware of the shortcomings of the current public-private partnership model. The study also sheds significant light on how these critical infrastructure partners can work effectively with each other in enhancing the existing model or in the creation of a new model.

## Limitations

Yin (2012) stated that a good use of theories will aid in delimiting a case study to its most effective design and that theory is essential is necessary in generalizing the results. In 2014, Yin stated that single case studies offered a poor basis with which to generalize a study's results. This is primarily because some researchers look at how the generalized results relate to the universe as a whole but case studies rely on analytic generalizations (2014). The research, while attempting to have a large population of participants, was only able to interview fifteen employees of Company XYZ. The collection of data was limited to the participants' understanding of security best practices, their identification, and the interworking's of Company XYZ.

The study focused on identifying suggested security best practices within Company XYZ. The researcher did not look at any other critical infrastructure partner organizations or other critical sector members. The study instead focused on an immature organization struggling to grasp the elements of identifying suggested security best practices. These limitations do open up additional research avenues but for the purposes of this study, it provides only a limited view on the critical infrastructure organizations as a whole.

# Recommendations

The study's findings, combined with the literature review, brought forth some interesting ways to identify suggested security best practices based on the themes presented in Chapter 4. A major recommendation that needs future research is on how organizations in each critical infrastructure sector as well as across sectors identify their suggested security best practices and how to share those affectively. Table 5 breaks down the eight themes found during the studies interviews and place recommendations around them.

Table 5

*Recommendations for Suggested Best Practice Identification*

| Observation | | Recommendation |
|---|---|---|
| Theme | Title | Case Study Recommendations |
| Theme 1 | Responsible Parties for Suggested Best Practice Identification | 1. Determine the effectiveness of the organizations security team to identify suggested security best practices.<br>2. Develop methods to ensure that the security team effectively communicates with internal business partners.<br>3. Provide senior management and the C-Suite the tools to aid in identify suggested security best practices. |
| Theme 2 | Senior Management Involvement and Knowledge | 1. Provide senior management and the C-Suite the necessary education on the identification of suggested security best practices.<br>2. Develop a formalized process to allow senior management and the C-Suite to gain more information from internal business partners than from the media or social media. |
| Theme 3 | Security Training | 1. Mandate role based security training to yield the best results in identifying suggested security best practices.<br>2. Facilitate periodic training incidents around the organizations roles, as it will allow for better adoption of suggested security best practices. |

Table 5 (Continued)

*Recommendations for Suggested Best Practice Identification*

| | Observation | Recommendation |
|---|---|---|
| Theme | Title | Case Study Recommendations |
| Theme 4 | Proactive Security | 1. Initiate proactive security measures to identify suggested security best practices.<br>2. Mandate security awareness training to promote proactive security to identify suggested security best practices. |
| Theme 5 | Security Assessments | 1. Management needs to bring in third party assessors to aid in identifying suggested security best practices.<br>2. Allow internal assessments to gain information on known processes.<br>3. Third party assessments bring in more overall best practices from working with other clients. |
| Theme 6 | Information Sharing with Partners | 1. Initiate communications with sector partners both within the organizations sector and with other DHS critical infrastructures partners.<br>2. Determine what is the acceptable level of sharing from the organization from a shareholder and liability standpoint.<br>3. Perform the necessary data scrubbing necessary to share and educate partners without allow new vulnerabilities within the organization. |
| Theme 7 | Future Preparation | 1. Mandate policies around identify suggested security best practices.<br>2. Senior management and C-Suite need to determine critical risks paths to remediate versus placing controls around.<br>3. Create policies on information sharing and participation in sharing forums. |
| Theme 8 | Alternative Methods | 1. Senior management and the C-Suite need to design policy allowing for the security cultural shift.<br>2. Mandate risk determinations around insider threat vectors and identify suggested security best practices to mitigate them.<br>3. Design a policy and usage around honeypots within the organization to gain an edge on adversaries. |

## Theme 1 Responsible Parties for Suggested Best Practice Identification

The recommendations provided by the interview participants in the determination of who should be responsible in the organization to identify the suggested security best practices were discussed within the first theme. The participants identified that it should be a function of the organization's security team and it is the security team's responsibility to effectively communicate those suggested best practices to the organization. The security team should also be the party responsible for providing the necessary tools to the senior leadership and C-Suite to help them aid in the identification of suggested security best practices. It was also determined that the security team should implement the suggested security best practices once those have been identified. There was also a slight agreement that the business should have the ability to help guide the security team in areas of the business that might be out of the realm of information technology.

## Theme 2 Senior Management Involvement and Knowledge

The second theme involved a discussion with the interview participants around the involvement and knowledge provided by the senior management team and C-Suite. The discussion determined that senior management and the C-Suite needed elements of a security education to aid them in identify suggested security best practices. To do this the participants felt that a formalized process was necessary to educate those members. This process could focus around social media and news outlets but also needed to involve regular discussions with the security team and business partners. An additional recommendation by participants was that the senior leadership team and C-Suite needed

to focus less on the dollars and cents and more on protecting the customers that allow
them to make that money and that the best start was education.

## Theme 3 Security Training

Security training was the focus of the third theme, and the study participants were
in complete agreement that role-based security training was the best practice. The
participants felt that an umbrella method of security training gave good information but is
likely to fall short and be easily forgotten. With a method of focusing training on roles of
individuals, the training would allow for the identification of new suggested best
practices as the training topics directly relate to the employee's day-to-day process. It was
also noted during the discussions that providing periodic incident training, such as
phishing attempts or social engineering calls, would allow for more adoption of security
policies. Finally, the conversations noted that adding connections to employees' home
life would be an added bonus that would allow the employee to better grasp some of the
more difficult security concepts.

## Theme 4 Proactive Security

The fourth theme centered on the ability of an organization that utilizes proactive
security to aid in identifying suggested security best practices. The participants felt
strongly that security awareness training is one of the most important aspects to
identifying suggested security best practices. If the awareness training was not effective
in getting the right message across to the employees the fear was that best practices
would not be identified and those that were identified might be overlooked or lost. The
other benefits that participants saw with a proactive security posture was that compliance

and regulatory issues were easier to implement and maintain. A proactive stance would keep the organization out of the news headlines because of a breach, hack, or loss of data.

## Theme 5 Security Assessments

Security assessments from an internal versus third party perspective were looked at in the fifth theme. The study participants felt that there was a benefit to a mixed approach towards security assessments and its benefits to identifying suggested security best practices. Third party assessors, while not knowing a lot about the internal environment, brought in a wealth of knowledge around the work performed with other clients in different critical infrastructure sectors. The participants stated that internal assessments were good in identifying suggested security best practices but there is an element of bias in the findings as those assessments only look at the organization and not industry best practices. The combination of both assessments allowed for a less biased approach and yielded the most suggested security best practices that would truly aid the organization in protecting its critical infrastructure.

## Theme 6 Information Sharing with Partners

Theme six yielded very interesting and mixed reviews from the study participants as it discussed the sharing of information with partners. While the participants all agreed that sharing information with critical infrastructure partners was extremely beneficial, they all had differing opinions on the extent and amount of sharing provided. The participants all felt that sharing with Department of Homeland Security critical infrastructure partners could yield industry leading best practices and better ways to secure critical information. It was determined that an acceptable level of sharing was necessary from a shareholder and liability standpoint.

There was also a consensus that the data needed to be scrubbed of critical points. This data scrubbing would allow other partners to learn from the vulnerability, hack or attack without giving the exact path the malicious individual took to initiate it or sustain it. In addition, it was recommended not to share any data that was exfiltrated, and if it was, to ensure that no legal liability was initiated. The final recommendation on theme six was that DHS needed to ensure that the infrastructure partners were properly checked to ensure that information shared could not be leaked or used against the organization. It was determined that this background checking would yield more communication and lead to the identification of more suggested security best practices that could be shared across sectors.

**Theme 7 Future Preparation**

The study participants were asked about what benefits or best practices could be identified if the organization prepared properly for the future in theme seven. The participants identified some very interesting perspectives. The participants felt that security policies and standards needed to mandate the usage of identified suggested best practices. The senior management and C-Suite also needed to be more actively involved in remediation of existing vulnerabilities and to aid in the creation of controls to mitigate identified risks where a suggested best practice has yet to be identified. A policy also needs to be drafted around information sharing and how the organization can participate in information sharing forums. The policy would allow for the identification of suggested best practices, allow for good information sharing, provide education to other sector members, and protect the organization's critical infrastructure and data from compromise.

**Theme 8 Alternative Methods**

The final theme looked to the participants to gain an idea of other alternative methods that could be utilized to aid in identifying suggested security best practices. The three main recommendations gained during this discussion focused on the senior management team and C-Suite taking a more active approach to identifying suggested security best practices within the organization. The second focused on mandating controls around the insider threat landscape and what suggested security best practices could be identified around that issue. The third main recommendation was the use of honeypots within the organization to lure attackers to determine how vulnerabilities are being exploited so that the organization can identify additional suggested security best practices.

The overarching recommendation was communication within the organization. These communications need to come from the senior management team and C-Suite to the organization's employees. It is also necessary for the organization to communicate effectively with information sharing forums, as this will allow for the success in identifying suggested best practices. There also needs to be continuous process improvements around existing security best practices but also in ways the organization can identify new suggested security best practices. Finally, the necessity of education around security best practices, role specific training, and keeping up to date on the threat landscape rounded out the recommendations.

The eight themes identified in this study provide recommendation on identifying suggested security best practices based on a single case study. Any company within a Department of Homeland Security determined critical infrastructure could take these recommendations and easily follow them to aid in the identification of their own suggested security best practices. These suggested recommendations need further research to determine their acceptability across critical infrastructure sectors as well as partners within the same sector. Furthermore, the study results contributed important and necessary knowledge to the field as they point to ways that an organization can identify suggested security best practices to aid in protecting its critical infrastructure.

**Recommendations for Future Research**

The body of literature surrounding the identification of suggested security best practices utilizing the public-private partnership model and frameworks designed using that model were non-existent when beginning this study. The study will build out the future literature and begin to fill in that lack of scholarly research; however, additional research will be necessary to continue building out the literature around this topic. The majority of Chapter 5 discusses several recommendations for future research.

Recommendations specific to future research in identifying suggested security best practices include expanding the research population. The population for this exploratory case study looked solely at Company XYZ contained within the Communications Sector of the Department of Homeland Security's seventeen critical infrastructure sectors. The research should look at other telecommunications companies like Company XYZ as well as other Communications Sector participants. This would benefit those critical infrastructure members as they look to further protect their critical infrastructure.

Additional research into how organizations are determined to participate within the information sharing forums is another area of interest. Research from the participants within Company XYZ noted several times the lack of wiliness to share detailed information on vulnerabilities and attack vectors to their organizations. It was noted that the Department of Homeland Security did not have any solid criteria around the protection of participating organizations that volunteered information. This also included any of the legal liabilities that an organization may come under by sharing critical information on attacks or losses of information.

Another future study would be into how security awareness programs aid organizations in identifying suggested security best practices. The participants from Company XYZ noted in several responses how important proper education of employees was necessary to identify suggested security best practices. There were also the discussions around the education necessary for the senior management team and C-Suite. Education was a running theme that could add a necessary element to understanding future security best practice identification.

Lastly, a study on how third party security assessments, used in conjunction with an organization's regulatory compliance efforts, help in identifying suggested security best practices. Many organizations within these critical infrastructure sectors are held accountable to regulatory elements such as the Payment Card Industry Data Security Standards (PCI DSS), Sarbanes-Oxley (SOX), Family Educational Rights and Privacy Act (FERPA), Federal Information Security Management Act (FISMA), and Health Insurance Portability and Accountability Act (HIPAA), to just name a few. The assessments that organization must undergo both internally and through the usage of external assessors can yield additional avenues to identifying suggested security best practices within an organization.

**Summary**

The problem that continuously motivated this study was the consensus that private and public sector partners lacked security best practices to protect critical infrastructure from cyberattack (Federal Register, 2013; IT SCC, 2013; McConnell, 2013; Wildman, 2013; Canfield and Ward, 2013; IT SCC, 2013; Rupy and Mayer, 2013; Chessen, Polk, Podey, Symons, and Harvie, 2013; Coffey, Srihari, and Scarpelli, 2013). The aim of this study was to determine how the security frameworks designed using the public-private partnership model aid in identifying suggested security best practices for a telecommunications provider's critical infrastructure within the United States. Thus, this study addressed the problem statement in that it showed there is not a complete lack of suggested security best practice identification. The study also showed that the usage of the current public-private partnership is effective.

The findings showed that there is room for improvement in identifying suggested security best practices. Although Company XYZ was utilizing security best practices that it had identified, it was determined through the interviews, that other existing sources were not being utilized to identify even more suggested security best practices. The public-private partnership method was not completely effective; it works and could perform better if some changes are made. Changes are necessary to improve on the model such as proper partner background checks and ensuring that sharing forums are secured to those cleared critical infrastructure partners. Another change could be on the ability to forgo legal liability or at the least institute anonymity around the organization(s) choosing to share information details that allow other partners to best protect themselves and identify their own security best practices.

This exploratory case study investigated the identification of suggested security best practices to protect critical infrastructure. To understand the phenomena, the researcher collected data to complete the literature review, direct and indirect observational data from participant interviews, and interview responses from fifteen employees from within Company XYZ, a critical infrastructure partner within the Communications Sector. The research goal was to determine how security frameworks designed utilizing the public-private partnership model aid in the identification of suggested security best practices for a telecommunications provider's critical infrastructure within the United States. This study was unique in that there is currently little to no academic research surrounding how security frameworks designed using the public-private partnership models aid in the identification of suggested security best practices as it relates to critical infrastructure protection of telecommunications providers. As stated earlier in this study, case study results are restricted to their usage within that specific case study and cannot be generalized to larger populations.

REFERENCES

Ahmad, R., & Yunos, Z. (2012). The application of mixed method in developing a cyber terrorism framework. *Journal of Information Security, 3*(3), 209-214. http://dx.doi.org/10.4236/jis.2012.33026

Ahmad, R., & Yunos, Z. (2012b). A dynamic cyber terrorism framework. *International Journal of Computer Science and Information Security, 10*(2), 149-158. Retrieved from http://www.docstoc.com/docs/116243605/A-Dynamic-Cyber-Terrorism-Framework

Ahmad, R., Yunos, Z., Sahib, S., & Yusoff, M. (2012). Perception on cyberterrorism: a focus group discussion approach. *Journal of Information Security, 3*(3), 231-237. Doi:10.4236/jis.2012.33029

Alcaraz, C. & Lopez, J. (2013, 04/01). Wide-area situational awareness for critical infrastructure protection. *Computer, 46*, 30-37. Retrieved from http://doi.ieeecomputersociety.org/10.1109/MC.2013.72

Alcaraz, C. & Zeadally, S. (2013). Critical control system protection in the 21$^{st}$ century. *Computer, 46*(10), 74-83. doi:10.1109/MC.2013.69

Avina, J. (2011). Public-private partnerships in the fight against crime: An emerging frontier in corporate social responsibility. *Journal of Financial Crime, 18*(3), 282-291. doi:http://dx.doi.org/10.1108/13590791111147505

Baines, L., & Chiarelott, L. (2010). Public/private partnerships: A trojan horse for higher education? *Journal of Computing in Higher Education, 22*(3), 153-161. doi:http://dx.doi.org/10.1007/s12528-010-9035-2

Bessani, A. N., Sousa, P., Correia, M., Neves, N. F., &Verissimo, P. (2008). The crutial way of critical infrastructure protection. *IEEE Security & Privacy, 6*(6), 44-51. http://dx.doi.org/10.1109/MSP.2008.158

Blair, J., Czaja, R. F., Blair, E. A. (2014). *Designing surveys: A guide to decisions and procedures.* Thousand Oaks, CA: SAGE Publications Inc.

Brechbuhl, H., Bruce, R., Dynes, S., & Johnson, M. (2010). Protecting critical information infrastructure: Developing cybersecurity policy. *Information Technology for Development, 16*(1), 83-91. Doi:10.1002/itdj.20096

Busch, N. E., & Givens, A. D. (2012). Public-private partnerships in homeland security: Opportunities and challenges. *Homeland Security Affairs, 8*(1). Retrieved from http://www.hsaj.org/?article=8.1.18

Caldeira, F. (2011). Trust based interdependency weighting for on-line risk monitoring in interdependent critical infrastructures. *2011 6th International Conference on Risks and Security of Internet and Systems (CRiSIS),* 1-7. Retrieved from http://doi.ieeecomputersociety.org/10.1109/CRiSIS.2011.6061545

Canfield, J., & Ward, J. (2013, April). Re: Notice of Inquiry – Incentives to adopt improved cybersecurity practices (Docket Number 130206115-3115-01), NTCA – The Rural Broadband Association. Retrieved from http://www.ntia.doc.gov/files/ntia/04.29.13_-_ntca_comments.pdf

Cavelty, M. D., &Suter, M. (2009). Public–Private Partnerships are no silver bullet: An expanded governance model for Critical Infrastructure Protection. *International Journal of Critical Infrastructure Protection, 2*(4), 179-187. http://dx.doi.org/10.1016/j.ijcip.2009.08.006.

Cellucci, T. A. (2010). Innovative public-private partnerships: A pathway to effectively

 solving problems. *U.S. Department of Homeland Security, Science and*

 *Technology Directorate*. Retrieved from

 http://www.dhs.gov/xlibrary/assets/st_innovative_public_private_partnerships_07

 10_version_2.pdf

Chessen, R., Polk, L., Podey, S. L., Symons, H. J., & Harvie, C. J. (2013, April). Re:

 Notice of Inquiry – Incentives to adopt improved cybersecurity practices (Docket

 Number 130206115-3115-01), The National Cable & Telecommunications

 Association. Retrieved from

 http://www.ntia.doc.gov/files/ntia/042913_ncta_comments.pdf

Clinton, L. (2005). What are you afraid of? Risks, roles and responsibilities in the public-

 private partnership to secure cyberspace. *Enterprise Risk Management and*

 *Governance Advisory Service Executive Update, 2*(15), 1-4. Retrieved from

 http://www.cutter.com/risk/fulltext/updates/2005/ermu0515.html

Clinton, L. (2011). A relationship on the rocks: Industry-government partnership for

 cyber defense. *Journal of Strategic Security, 4*(2), 97-111. doi:10.5038/1944-

 0472.4.2.6

Coffey, D., Srihari, D., & Scarpelli, B. (2013, April). Re: Notice of Inquiry – Incentives

 to adopt improved cybersecurity practices (Docket Number 130206115-3115-01),

 Telecommunications Industry Association. Retrieved from

 http://www.ntia.doc.gov/files/ntia/tia_comments_042913.pdf

Creswell, J. W. (2012). *Educational research: Planning, conducting, and evaluating quantitative and qualitative research.* Boston, MA: Pearson Education Inc.

Daniel, M. (2014, July 2). Talking cybersecurity [Web log post]. Retrieved from http://www.whitehouse.gov/blog/2014/07/02/talking-cybersecurity

Daniel, M. (2014, May 22). Assessing cybersecurity regulations [Web log post]. Retrieved from http://www.whitehouse.gov/blog/2014/05/22/assessing-cybersecurity-regulations

Daniel, M. (2014, April 10). Getting serious about information sharing for cybersecurity [Web log post]. Retrieved from http://www.whitehouse.gov/blog/2014/04/10/getting-serious-about-information-sharing-cybersecurity

Daniel, M. (2014, February 18). Launch of the cybersecurity framework –what's next? [Web log post]. Retrieved from http://www.whitehouse.gov/blog/2014/02/18/launch-cybersecurity-framework-what-s-next

Daniel, M. (2013, August 6). Incentives to support adoption of the cybersecurity framework [Web log post]. Retrieved from http://www.whitehouse.gov/blog/2013/08/06/incentives-support-adoption-cybersecurity-framework

Daniel, M. (2013, February 13). Improving the security of the nation's critical

    infrastructure [Web log post]. Retrieved from

    http://www.whitehouse.gov/blog/2013/02/13/improving-security-nation-s-critical-

    infrastructure

Daniel, M. (2012, August 1). Collaborative and cross-cutting approaches to

    cybersecurity [Web log post]. Retrieved from

    http://www.whitehouse.gov/blog/2012/08/01/collaborative-and-cross-cutting-

    approaches-cybersecurity

Federal Register, Department of Commerce. (2013). Incentives to adopt improved

    cybersecurity practices (Docket Number 130206115-3115-01). Retrieved from

    http://www.ntia.doc.gov/files/ntia/publications/cybersecurity_noi_03282013.pdf

Gaffney, F. J. (2014, September 3). Will ISIS strike America's achilles heel? Breitbart.

    http://www.breitbart.com/Big-Peace/2014/09/03/Will-ISIS-Strike-Americas-

    Achilles-Heel

Garcia, G. (2006). Forging a public-private partnership: The "wonk-free" approach to

    cyber security. *Cutter IT Journal: The Journal of Information Technology*

    *Management, 19*(5), 31-35. Retrieved from

    http://www.cutter.com/itjournal/fulltext/2006/05/itj0605g.html

Garvin, M. J. (2010). Enabling Development of the Transportation Public-Private

    Partnership Market in the United States. *Journal of Construction Engineering &*

    *Management, 136*(4), 402-411. doi:10.1061/(ASCE)CO.1943-7862.0000122

Garvin, M. J. (2012). Are Public–Private partnerships effective infrastructure development strategies? Paper presented at the *CME 25: Conference Construction Management and Economics: Past, Present and Future: 16th-18th July 2007,* University of Reading, England. 357.

Garvin, M. J. & Bosso, D. (2008). Assessing the effectiveness of infrastructure public-private partnership programs and projects. *Public Works Management & Policy, 13*(2), 162-176. doi:10.1177/1087724X08323845

Geer, D. (2013). Resolved: The Internet is no place for critical infrastructure. *Communications of the ACM, 56*(6), 48-53. doi:10.1145/2461256.2461273

George, T. (2011). The digital threat: Cyberattacks put critical infrastructure under fire. *Risk Management, 58*(8), 26-29. Retrieved from http://www.questia.com/magazine/1G1-269689924/the-digital-threat-cyberattacks-put-critical-infrastructure

Givens, A. D., &Busch, N.E. (2013). Realizing the promise of public-private partnerships in U.S. critical infrastructure protection. *International Journal of Critical Infrastructure Protection, 6*(1), 39-50. http://dx.doi.org/10.1016/j.ijcip.2013.02.002.

Glennon, M. J. (2012). State-level cybersecurity. *Policy Review,* (171), 85-102. Retrieved from http://www.questia.com/library/journal/1G1-280967312/state-level-cybersecurity

Goel, S. (2011). Cyberwarfare: Connecting the dots in cyber intelligence. *Communications of the ACM, 54*(8), 132-140. doi:http://doi.acm.org/10.1145/1978542.1978569

Grossman, S. A. (2012). Public-Private Partnerships: The emerging role of partnership governance. *Public Performance & Management Review, 35*(4), 575-577. http://dx.doi.org/10.2753/PMR1530-9576350400

Hall, C. (2012). Security of the internet and the known unknowns. *Communications of the ACM, 55*(6), 35-37. doi:http://doi.acm.org/10.1145/2184319.2184332

Information Technology Sector Coordinating Council (IT SCC) (2013, March). Re: Notice of Inquiry – Incentives to adopt improved cybersecurity practices (Docket Number 130206115-3115-01), Information Technology Sector Coordinating Council. Retrieved from http://www.ntia.doc.gov/files/ntia/2013-04-29_-_it_scc_response.pdf

Intelligence and National Security Alliance (INSA). (2000). Addressing cyber security through public-private partnership: An analysis of existing models. Retrieved from https://www.insaonline.org/i/d/a/Resources/Addressing_Cyber_Security.aspx

International Radiotelegraph Conference - Berlin (1906). International wireless telegraph convention concluded between Germany, the United States of America, Argentina, Austria, Hungary, Belgium, Brazil, Bulgaria, Chile, Denmark, Spain, France, Great Britain, Greece, Italy, Japan, Mexico, Monaco, Norway, the Netherlands, Persia, Portugal, Romania, Russia, Sweden, Turkey, and Uruguay. Washington, Government Printing Office, 1907. Retrieved from https://archive.org/stream/internationalrad00interich#page/n3/mode/2up

Katzan, H. (2011). Review of the cyberspace policy and trusted identity documents. *The Review of Business Information Systems, 15*(2), 43-49. Retrieved from http://connection.ebscohost.com/c/articles/60639375/review-cyberspace-policy-trusted-identity-documents

Kshetri, N. & Murugesan, S. (2013). EU and US cybersecurity strategies and their impact on businesses and consumers. *Computer, 46*(10), 84-88. Doi:10.1109/MC.2013.350

Li, R. & Unger, E. A. (1995). Security issues with TCP/IP. *SIGAPP Applied Computing Review* 3(1), 6-13. DOI=10.1145/214310.214313 http://doi.acm.org/10.1145/214310.214313

Maughan, D. (2010). The need for a national cybersecurity research and development agenda. *Communications of the ACM, 53*(2), 29-31. doi:10.1145/1646353.1646365

McConnell, J. M. (2013, April). Re: Notice of Inquiry – Incentives to adopt improved cybersecurity practices (Docket Number 130206115-3115-01), Booz Allen Hamilton. Retrieved from http://www.ntia.doc.gov/files/ntia/bah_response_042913_final.pdf

McNamara, J. M. (2013). *Protecting New York's infrastructure: Improving overall safety and security through new partnerships and concentration on planning, engineering and design* (Masters Thesis, Naval Postgraduate School). Retrieved from http://calhoun.nps.edu/public/bitstream/handle/10945/38984/13Dec_McNamara_John.pdf?sequence=1

Meidute, I. & Paliulis, N. K. (2011). Feasibility study of public-private partnership. *International Journal of Strategic Property Management, 15*(3), 257-274. doi:10.3846/1648715X.2011.617860

Meltzoff, J. (2010). *Critical thinking about research: Psychology and related fields.* Washington, DC: American Physiological Association.

National Institute of Standards and Technology. (2014). *Framework for Improving Critical Infrastructure Cybersecurity.* Retrieved from http://www.nist.gov/cyberframework/upload/cybersecurity-framework-021214-final.pdf

Newmeyer, K. P. (2012). Who should lead U.S. cybersecurity efforts? *Prism 3*(2), 115-126. Retrieved from http://cco.dodlive.mil/files/2014/02/prism115-126_newmeyer.pdf

Obama, B. (2012, July 23). Taking the cyberattack threat seriously [Web log post]. Retrieved from http://www.whitehouse.gov/blog/2012/07/23/taking-cyberattack-threat-seriously

Parsons, C., & Safdar, M. (2011). Defending cyberspace: The view from Washington. *The Brown Journal of World Affairs, 18*(1), 49-55. Retrieved from http://heinonline.org/HOL/LandingPage?handle=hein.journals/brownjwa18&div=8&id=&page=

Podbregar, I. & Podbregar, M. F. (2012). Critical infrastructure and internal controls. *2012 IEEE/ACM International Conference on Advances in Social Networks Analysis and Mining,* 858-862. http://dx.doi.org/10.1109/ASONAM.2012.155

Ridley, G. (2011). National security as a corporate social responsibility: Critical infrastructure resilience. *Journal of Business Ethics, 103*(1), 111-125. Retrieved from http://link.springer.com/article/10.1007%2Fs10551-011-0845-6

Rupy, K., & Mayer, R. (2013, April). Re: Notice of Inquiry – Incentives to adopt improved cybersecurity practices (Docket Number 130206115-3115-01), The United States Telecom Association. Retrieved from http://www.ntia.doc.gov/files/ntia/ustelecom-comments-2013-04-29-final.pdf

Rutkowski, A. M. (2010). Lessons from the first great cyberwar era. *Info, 12*(1), 5-9. doi:10.1108/14636691011015330

Saldana, J. (2009). *The Coding Manual for Qualitative Researchers.* Thousand Oaks, CA: Sage Publications Inc.

Salkind, N. J. (2012). *Exploring research.* Boston, MA: Pearson Education Inc.

Schmidt, H. A. (2012, May 21). Partnership developments in cybersecurity [Web log post]. Retrieved from http://www.whitehouse.gov/blog/2012/05/21/partnership-developments-cybersecurity

Schmidt, H. A. (2012, January 26). Legislation to address the growing danger of cyber threats [Web log post]. Retrieved from http://www.whitehouse.gov/blog/2012/01/26/legislation-address-growing-danger-cyber-threats

Schmidt, H. A. (2011, October 28). The time is ripe for cybersecurity legislation [Web log post]. Retrieved from http://www.whitehouse.gov/blog/2011/10/28/time-ripe-cybersecurity-legislation

Stebbins, R. A. (2001). *Exploratory Research in the Social Sciences.* Thousand Oaks, CA: SAGE Publications, Inc. http://dx.doi.org/10.4135/9781412984249

Stephan, R. B. (2006). Cyber risk management: The need for effective public and private partnership. *Cutter IT Journal: The Journal of Information Technology Management, 19*(1), 6-10. Retrieved from http://www.cutter.com/content/itjournal/fulltext/2006/01/itj0601b.html

Tofan, D. C., Andrei, M. L., & Dinca, L. M. (2012). Cyber security policy. A methodology for determining a national cyber-security alert level. *Informatica Economica, 16*(2), 103-115. Retrieved from http://revistaie.ase.ro/content/62/11%20-%20Tofan.pdf

Trope, R. L. & Humes, S. J. (2013, 03/01). By executive order: Delivery of cyber intelligence imparts cyber responsibilities. *IEEE Security & Privacy*, 11, 63-67. Retrieved from http://doi.ieeecomputersociety.org/10.1109/MSP.2013.29

United States Department of Homeland Security (HSPD-7). (2003). *Homeland Security Presidential Directive 7: Critical Infrastructure Identification, Prioritization and Protection.* Retrieved from http://www.dhs.gov/homeland-security-presidential-directive-7

United States Department of Homeland Security. (2010). *Communications Sector Specific Plan: An Annex to the National Infrastructure Protection Plan.* Retrieved from http://www.dhs.gov/xlibrary/assets/nipp-ssp-communications-2010.pdf

United States Department of Homeland Security (NIPP). (2013). *National Infrastructure Protection Plan.* Retrieved from http://www.dhs.gov/national-infrastructure-protection-plan

United States Department of Homeland Security (EO-13636). (2013, March). *Executive Order (EO) 13636 Improving Critical Infrastructure Cybersecurity: Integration Task Force.* Retrieved from http://www.dhs.gov/sites/default/files/publications/nppd/CSC/ITF%20Fact%20Sheet%20March%202013.pdf

United States Department of Homeland Security (EO-13636). (2013, June). *Executive Order (EO) 13636 Improving Critical Infrastructure Cybersecurity.* Retrieved from http://www.dhs.gov/sites/default/files/publications/dhs-eo13636-analytic-report-cybersecurity-incentives-study.pdf

United States Department of Homeland Security, (2014). *Our Mission.* Retrieved from http://www.dhs.gov/our-mission

United States White House (PPD-21). (2013, February). *Presidential Policy Directive: Critical Infrastructure Security and Resilience (PPD-21).* Retrieved from http://www.whitehouse.gov/the-press-office/2013/02/12/presidential-policy-directive-critical-infrastructure-security-and-resil

Westby, J. (2012). Congress needs to go back to school on cyber legislation. *Forbes,* http://www.forbes.com/sites/jodywestby/2012/08/13/congress-needs-to-go-back-to-school-on-cyber-legislation/

Wildman, S. S. (2013, May). Re: Notice of Inquiry – Incentives to adopt improved cybersecurity practices (Docket Number 130206115-3115-01), Federal Communications Commission. Retrieved from http://www.ntia.doc.gov/files/ntia/20130502_fcc_response.pdf

Yin, R. K. (2014). *Case study research: Design and Methods.* Thousand Oaks, CA: SAGE Publications, Inc.

Yin, R. K. (2012). *Applications of case study research.* Thousand Oaks, CA: SAGE Publications, Inc.

## APPENDIX A: KEY LITERATURE REVIEW SEARCH TERMS

- Public-Private Partnership
- Critical Infrastructure Protection
- Department of Homeland Security
- Cybersecurity Policy
- Executive Order
- Presidential Policy Directive
- Cybersecurity Framework
- Equilibrium Model
- National Infrastructure Protection Plan
- Effectiveness
- Communications Sector

## APPENDIX B: LITERATURE SEARCH

| Key Word Search | Peer Reviewed Works Reviewed | Germinal Works Reviewed | Books Reviewed | Dissertations Reviewed |
|---|---|---|---|---|
| Critical Infrastructure | | | | |
| Public-Private Partnership | 184 | 15 | 0 | 9 |
| Critical Infrastructure Protection | 83 | 0 | 0 | 2 |
| Department of Homeland Security | 28 | 0 | 0 | 0 |
| Cybersecurity Policy and Framework | 22 | 0 | 0 | 0 |
| National Infrastructure Protection Plan | 19 | 0 | 0 | 0 |
| Executive Order & Presidential Policy Directive | 8 | 0 | 0 | 0 |
| Effectiveness | 51 | 0 | 0 | 8 |
| Communications Sector | 9 | 0 | 0 | 0 |
| Research Methodology | | | | |
| Qualitative Analysis | 27 | 12 | 6 | 0 |
| Quantitative Analysis | 11 | 7 | 3 | 0 |
| Total Documents Reviewed (504) | 442 | 34 | 9 | 19 |

APPENDIX C:  METHODOLOGY MAP

## Research Methodology Map

### Qualitative Case Study Research
- Effectiveness of the public-private partnership model for security best practice design
- Extend knowledge of critical infrastructure protection using the partnership model

### Literature Review
- Review seminal and significant research around critical infrastructure protection, the public-private partnership model, and security best practices
- Identify gap in research surrounding security best practice design

### Pilot Study
- Affirm validity and reliability of measurement instrument and experiment procedure
- Facilitate pilot study
- Adjust interview questions as necessary

### Data Collection
- Collect interview answers and artifacts for the cast study
- Use:
  - Case Study Protocol

### Data Analysis
- Enter data into the Case Study Database
- Apply Case Study Coding to the Data
  - First Phase Coding
  - Second Phase Coding

### Data Interpretation and Reporting
- Interpret case study data and results
- Discuss trends and potential meanings
- Determine recommendation for future research based on findings
- Submit final dissertation to Capitol College

# APPENDIX D: CASE STUDY PROTOCOL

Outline –PPP Model for Security Best Practice Identification

1. Introduction to the case study and purpose of protocol

    a. Case study questions

    b. Case study objectives

    c. Theoretical framework for the case study

    d. Role of protocol in guiding the case study investigator

2. Data collection procedures

    a. Name of the site for the case study and participants

    b. Case study preparation

    c. Chain of custody of the data

3. Case study database

    a. Database plan

    b. Coding framework

4. Case study coding procedures

    a. Coding procedures after the artifacts are collected

        i. Primary Coding

5. Outline of the case study report

    a. Introduction to the case study

    b. Phases of the case study

    c. Outcome of the case study

    d. Analysis of the case study artifacts

6. Case study questions

    a. Describe the current usage of the public-private partnership model in designing suggested security best practices.

    b. Do critical infrastructure employees understand that they are a critical infrastructure?

    c. Do critical infrastructure employees understand the National Infrastructure Protection Plan?

    d. Do critical infrastructure employees use security best practices to protect the critical infrastructure they work for?

    e. Does the pubic-private partnership model aid in identifying suggested security best practices for critical infrastructure?

## APPENDIX F: INTERVIEW QUESTIONS FOR CASE STUDY

1.  Who in Company XYZ is responsible for developing and implementing organization-wide cybersecurity protective measures (devices, policy, etc.) and is this the right or wrong person, explain?

2.  How is Company XYZ's senior leadership informed about cyber risk and its impact on the overall business and is the input gained from their expertise/experience utilized to identify security best practices?

3.  What benefits could Company XYZ gain by utilizing role-specific training around security awareness, incident response, and threat assessment? Will this aid in identifying security best practices?

4.  As part of Company XYZ's proactive security posture, what benefits could the organization gain by determining, reviewing, and protecting critical data/systems?

5.  How does self-assessment of cyber protection capabilities aid Company XYZ and/or would a third party or best practice sharing system be more suited to aid in the identification of security best practices?

6.  To aid in identifying security best practices should Company XYZ actively participate in information sharing forums with other critical infrastructure partners and what benefits can be gained by doing so?

7.  Would the sharing of both attempted and successful intrusions attempts on Company XYZ with other critical infrastructure partners, through an information-sharing forum, lend itself to identifying security best practices to protect Company XYZ from similar attacks in the future and is this sharing a good idea?

8. Do you think that information sharing with other critical infrastructure partners could allow Company XYZ to be more vulnerable to cyberattack? Why or why not?

9. Do you think that proper preparation for future incidents, including information sharing, will aid Company XYZ's effort to properly identify security best practices to protect it? Why or why not?

10. What other methods can Company XYZ utilize to aid in identifying security best practices to protect its critical infrastructure?

APPENDIX G: TEST RESULTS

| Participants | Interview Questions | | | | | | | | | |
|---|---|---|---|---|---|---|---|---|---|---|
| | 1 | 2 | 3 | 4 | 5 | 6 | 7 | 8 | 9 | 10 |
| P1 | | | | | | | | | | |
| P2 | | | | | | | | | | |
| P3 | | | | | | | | | | |
| P4 | | | | | | | | | | |
| P5 | | | | | | | | | | |
| P6 | | | | | | | | | | |
| P7 | | | | | | | | | | |
| P8 | | | | | | | | | | |
| P9 | | | | | | | | | | |
| P10 | | | | | | | | | | |
| P11 | | | | | | | | | | |
| P12 | | | | | | | | | | |
| P13 | | | | | | | | | | |
| P14 | | | | | | | | | | |
| P15 | | | | | | | | | | |

X - Provided researcher with a satisfactory answer to the question.

Y - Provided researcher with an unsatisfactory answer to the question.

www.ingramcontent.com/pod-product-compliance
Lightning Source LLC
LaVergne TN
LVHW060143070326
832902LV00018B/2935